Lora Lee Parrott

# Come Over to My House

# Come Over to My House

## A Guide to Christian Hospitality
### *with over 60 recipes*
*by Lora Lee Parrott*

**Warner Press**
**Anderson, Indiana**

Credits:
*Illustrated by Bonnie Snellenberger*
*Cover photos by Audrey Nilsen*
Unless otherwise noted, all Scripture quotations are from the Holy Bible:
Revised Standard Version and King James Version. Used by permission.

# Contents

# Ease in Entertaining

# Pleasure in Raising the Children

# Matters of Personal Privilege

# New Horizons and Fresh Resources

*Dedicated*
*to*
*Dorothy Friesen*
*whose*
*Christian hospitality*
*has inspired me and many other women*
*to appreciate*
*gracious entertaining.*

# Introduction

The Gaither Trio was to give an evening concert at a Christian college in the East. Our three small children were with us, and it was late afternoon before we arrived. We were all tired from the trip and the baby was fussy. We were directed to the college president's home where a beautiful, formal luncheon for the faculty was just being cleared; the last of the well-dressed guests were still talking in small circles around the room.

That's when I first met Lora Lee Parrott. She greeted us and without any hint of frustration or pressure, made us feel welcome, and introduced us to the faculty guests with clues to the interests and achievements of each.

As natural conversation began, she pulled me to one side. "I know what it's like to be a young mother," she told me, "and I know you must be exhausted. Would you like to slip away and find a place to quiet the baby?"

I was relieved at the offer. Before I knew it, Lora Lee had put a cold drink in my hand and had given Amy some milk and cookies. We found ourselves upstairs away from the crowd, and soon both Amy and the baby were sound asleep for a much needed nap.

Since that day I've watched Lora Lee feed crowds or hostess intimate groups with the same ease. I have sipped her icy, coffee ice cream slush* before a formal candlelit dinner at Christmas; I've sat at her kitchen table while she scrubbed the stove; I've watched her turn a catered, campground dining hall buffet into a lovely event.

I have found Lora Lee to be gracious and elegant, but also human and imperfect. I've watched her deal with dignitaries

---

*French Iced Coffee; see chapter 9.*

in the parlor and the family dog on the back porch, and I've discovered that her life—in spite of the fact that she's lived in parsonages and college presidents' mansions—is much like mine: hectic, delightful, pressured, confusing, and surprisingly joyful.

The secrets she shares in this book are what we all look for: ways to cope! At a time when women are supposed to be all their grandmothers were and all their daughters hope to be, most of us feel like superwoman caught in a blender. Lora Lee doesn't pretend that she has never felt pressure, experienced failure, known exhaustion, or exploded in frustration. Instead, she tells what God has taught her in all the contradictory circumstances of her life and how to treat all these "imposters just the same."

*Gloria Gaither*

# Delight in
# Keeping the Home

*By wisdom a house is built*
*And through understanding it is established.*
*Through knowledge its rooms are filled*
*With rare and beautiful treasures.*
*—Proverbs 24:3, 4 (NIV)*

# Come Over to My House

## Chapter One

CLARE Booth Luce made her long career more illustrious because she learned to read people—not like a book, but as people. During her long career as a Broadway playwright, wife of *Time* magazine's Henry Luce, and America's ambassador to Italy, Mrs. Luce put high priority on judging people by looking into their eyes. She said, "I can immediately tell more about a person by looking full into his eyes than I can by looking at his calling card or reading his resume'." A calling card will announce the role a person is playing in the culture and the resume' will outline in succinct form what the person has done thus far in life, but the eyes reveal what he or she is like as a human being. It has been said that the eyes are the "windows of the soul."

In my role as a pastor's wife, I have visited many times with many people at the door of the church, in the foyer, and sometimes for privacy, in an empty classroom. I have shaken hands and greeted as many as five hundred people before the Sunday night service by walking slowly up and down the aisles and shaking hands with people who looked up to meet my eyes with theirs. I built up a clientele of people who developed expectations concerning my Sunday night greetings. I felt good about myself because of the number of people I could call by name and I got something of a small reputation for it.

I suppose I have made and received thousands of phone calls from men, women, and young people in the church. But I never felt that I could really know and understand people until I visited with them in their own homes. Seeing where they lived and how they lived was like looking into the eyes of their soul. Maybe that is why I would like to say to you, "Come over to my house." If you want to know me, you need to see the places where I have lived. The houses I have lived

**If you want to know me, come over to my house. In the home you and I reveal who we really are.**

in are not as important as the attitudes I have had toward them. But taken together—the places I have lived in and my attitudes toward them—and you have some of the most important building blocks in the structure of what makes me what I am.

I have taken great numbers of people through my home a few at a time and sometimes in large groups. The trip is imaginary; it's a magic carpet experience with many vicarious and substitutionary overtones. Although we may begin the visit, leaving on our flying machine from the melancholy setting of some nondescript motel meeting room or a gathering place in a church fellowship hall, we never return without our understanding each other better. If you want to know me, *come over to my house.* It's in the home that you and I reveal who we really are. Our spiritual and cultural values are better reflected in our homes than they are in our public appearances at church.

I really do want you to come over to my house. But first of all, I have a problem about which house. Les, my loving husband and best friend, started married life with me in a three-room student apartment with the tiniest bathroom and kitchen you could ever imagine. There was no provision for heat in two of the important places in the apartment— bathroom and kitchen—and very little in our other two rooms. But here is the place where our married love began to grow. In these little rooms, I began learning how to adjust to him and he to me, the surest sign of a secure love.

**The rooms were larger than they really needed to be.**

In our first full-time pastorate, we inherited a huge house by our standards. The rooms were larger than they really needed to be. But the congregation built the big house as a partial answer for meeting the needs of a gathering place for social purposes. I was expected to volunteer our house and my services for all kinds of church social events, including class parties, sit-down dinners, showers, and the home away from home for all the evangelists, missionaries, and other special visitors. Lots of people came over to my house in Kelso and sometimes, as a prospective young mother, and later with a baby, I was overwhelmed.

In Flint, the parsonage, which was literally attached to the church, was made of cinder blocks, plastered on the inside and stuccoed against the heat and cold on the outside. The walls stayed hot in the summer and cold in the winter. Since the four bedrooms had no closets, we put two of them together and dared to have a little dressing room. But that block house provided us with a great living experience. It was here that our second son was born, and we were waiting for the third when we finally moved on eight years later. In this block house we really became a family, sometimes rough and tumbled, and sometimes sensitive and quiet—but our evolving love was still growing. Les earned his Ph.D. at Michigan State while we lived in this house, and I felt I was building a strong self-image following the publication of two successful books and a *Ladies Home Journal* article. I knew who I was. We felt good enough about each other to borrow the money and make our first Christmas trip to England from that house.

The third boy was born in the Bellevue Hospital and taken home to an old refurbished home with a poor man's view of Lake Washington and Seattle beyond. Kelso, which was mercifully brief, was a tough interim. But like other chilly, uncomfortable circumstances in life, this experience had its good times, and in all, it helped bring us closer together.

The parsonage in Kirkland was only a brief stopover—twenty months—en route to the house that was really to become home for seven beautiful years in Portland. All of the studies on the happiness of married couples indicate the best years of life are when the children are all home. They are not easy years, but they overflow with the stuff that makes memories. Our best family years were in a suburban plat house, several inconvenient miles from the church, where our family room dining area had a gorgeous view across the valley to Mount Hood. The shopping center was at the bottom of the hill and the school at the top. It took two cars to keep us going and all the money we could muster. Money for the needs of boys growing up was a conscious or unconscious concern through these years. It seemed like every decision was made with an eye on the checkbook. It was during these years that Les turned over all of the family finances to me and I learned a lot in a hurry about money. But this scene was one happy experience that lasted for seven beautiful years.

Then came the first college president's home, a big old New England house with a predictable floor plan. With a big central hallway and stairwell upstairs and down, there were four bedrooms up with one-half of the downstairs divided between kitchen and dining room, and the other half turned into a living room. It was a beautiful plan we later copied in building a house. We made the attic into a third level boys' town, put two bedrooms together for a large bedroom and closet-dressing area, and settled in for five wonderful years. Here in Quincy, we watched two boys become men while we dealt with our own secret sin of parental pride.

And now we are back where we started from, only a few blocks from the student apartment where we began our marriage. The high-pillared front on our new president's house is more impressive than it needs to be. But the house is just right, not too large or too small, too ornate or too plain, and in just the right place on the corner of the campus where it belongs. Here people have been invited over to our house both in small groups and in great numbers—as many as five or six hundred at a time—for a walk-through during the freshmen reception each fall.

Our youngest boy graduated this year and was married this summer. This means Les and I are really back where we started, looking across the breakfast table at each other with no children as a buffer between us. Frankly, we're looking forward to it.

I want to take you back now to our house in Quincy where the inspiration of two presidents of the United States—John Adams and his son John Quincy—still lingers. But first I need to say something to you about why I want you to come over to my house.

I am not a philosopher, not even a very good writer. I publish books because I like the process and the fulfillment of having done it, not because I think I'm good. And when I compare myself to my husband, I am not really a very deep thinker, although I can think faster than he does. He is forever asking those interminable questions with answers I already know. He's cerebral and he says I'm intuitive. He's right brained and I am left brained—or is it the other way around? But our home is one place where I express myself best. Other women paint, work for pay, or become house-wives. None of these challenges turns me on. But I do love to make a home and then invite people to come over to my house. I love decorating, although I'm always pressed for enough time and money to do things right. I collect outstanding recipes and publish them. But many of my best friends are better cooks than I am. I love quiet times at home with the doors closed and the blinds drawn. But what I enjoy most is the fun and fellowship of having the right number of compatible people over to my house for an evening of tasty food and wholesome conversation. I don't like games. But I do like people and stimulating talk around the dining table, or for that matter, the kitchen dinette.

It's Christian to open our homes to both friends and strangers. Jesus was forever being entertained in the homes of his friends, both for meals and as an overnight house guest. Inviting people over can be a ministry. For years, Les held the church board meetings in our home so that I could make the board members feel comfortable in receiving our hospitality. I now do the same thing with the college trustees and their wives—and I love it.

**It's Christian to open our homes to both friends and strangers.**

Les says, "The best meetings are those without an agenda." And I guess that is what Christian hospitality means to me. It's bringing the people together without an agenda.

I have poured over each of these pages with many hours of loving concern. It wouldn't take so long if I were a better writer. But I have strived to give you some inspiring glimpses into our house, hoping what you see and feel will turn into a higher level of understanding and appreciation for your own home as a means of Christian hospitality for your own family first, and then for your expanding circle of friends and people you would like for friends.

It's not the house that counts, but our attitude toward it that makes any home you or I have the happiest place in our lives. So, come over to my house. I love it and I think you will, too.

# Backdoor Hospitality

## Chapter Two

IN the nonverbal language of household architecture, lots of back doors, which open into the family kitchens of America, send out welcome signals totally unfamiliar to most front entrances. A big, heavy, ornate entrance may be impressive from the street, but it is just an expensive way to say, "I am a barrier that separates you from the hospitality of this home." In many communities this entrance barrier is necessary and must be heavily secured, but it is still a barrier.

However, in lots of family residences, kitchen doors in the back of the house are another matter. Many of them have taken the b-a-r out of b-a-r-r-i-e-r by using see-through glass, dutch doors, and a variety of decorative screen doors. These doors are usually secured, but not in the formidable way of most front entrances. The hospitable smells of the kitchen often welcome the backdoor visitor. Remnants of ongoing family activity linger, highly visible around kitchen doors. Garbage pails, tired brooms standing in protective corners, muddy boots cluttering the steps, and an empty case of pop bottles between the door and the driveway tell their own stories about real people inside.

There's even a difference in the kinds of people who come to the back door. Sales people, formal visitors, and pollsters are among those who frequent front entrances. They ring, step back politely, and wait to see what kind of reception they are going to get. But people who have already penetrated the hospitality barrier just naturally come to the kitchen door. This roster includes friends who announce themselves with an "Anybody home?" while they knock or ring the bell knowing the welcome mat is already out. Neighborhood kids come to the kitchen door because they know very well that everybody lives in the back of the house. Service people come to the back door because they have been sent for and their welcome mat of sorts is already in place.

Front entrances often open into formal hallways or vestibules that usually lead to socially cold, seldom used parlors or living rooms, while back doors often open into the warmth of the kitchen and the family living area that exudes welcome with its smells and sights and sounds.

I guess this is why I have always liked kitchen doors and have tried to prepare them for the frequent visitors who come over to my house.

In our house I've staked out the kitchen as my domain. I've used the breadboard as a writing desk for manuscripts. In the kitchen I learned to cook, talk on the telephone, and supervise the children all at the same time.

Les made many pastoral telephone calls from the kitchen table. These calls provoked a lot of spiritual conversation between him and me and became a factor in drawing us together spiritually. I'm much more mystical in my religion than he is. I worry about unanswerable questions related to spiritual healing, whose wife will she be in the resurrection, and what kinds of bodies will we have in heaven.

Les says he leaves all of that to God and he concerns himself with how to live the Christian life and what kinds of attitudes are consistent with the Christian faith and life of holiness. He lives by grace and practices a higher level of unconditional forgiveness and a more guilt-free way of thinking than I do. I can't help it—maybe it's my Indiana roots, but I'm more concerned than he is about how to keep the law and especially how others should keep it. I don't want to be judgmental but too often I am. Maybe this is why he goes to sleep the minute his head hits the pillow and I lie awake trying to resolve the unfinished issues of the day. He and I have always needed lots of time to talk with each other, and some of these best talks have been in the kitchen. When we talk in the kitchen, he's in my territory and I think it gives me an edge and the confidence I need.

I think every woman needs to do something to make her kitchen uniquely her own. I've done this with a profuse distribution of flowers and plants, by using brass pots and pans as the dominant decorating motif, and by making it my office. But one of the most interesting things I ever did was to paper the ceiling of an old house with a wall covering that featured large yellow and orange flowers.

We had just moved to New England from the West Coast and the continuing challenge to adjust was formidable for me and the whole family. Driving in Boston was a nightmare to the uninitiated. The houses were old beyond belief, at least from our western ranch-style perspective. We weren't ready for the level of neighborhood crime and vandalism that most people in our area seemed to accept as the norm. Brazen thieves took our boys' bicycles the first night we stayed in our new home. The police warned us about probable retaliation if we were too vigorous in trying to locate the missing bikes among the neighborhood children.

It was probably from culture shock that I instructed the decorators to find me paper with big flowers. I wanted synthetic sunshine guaranteed to make the kitchen the happiest atmosphere in the house. When the paperhanger measured for the big yellow and orange pattern I had chosen, I told him to include the ceiling.

He blanched and said, "You don't put that kind of paper on the ceiling, ma'am."

Ordinarily I would have backed away and let him dominate me. I was already coping with a house that was 7 percent off true measure in every room upstairs and down. The man who had built the place a generation before had served as his own architect and builder, choosing to follow the property lines instead of a compass setting. We had already put coach lights around the house to help dispel our fear of the darkness and with my husband's support, I had run a red carpet from the sidewalk up the steep steps to the front door and now I wanted a kitchen that was mine—uniquely mine.

Just then Les came through the back door from the campus and I told him what I wanted to do—to put the big print on the kitchen ceiling. I explained how it would do something for the back entrance and bring everybody who came through the back door directly into a world of manufactured sunshine. And Les responded just as I knew he would. He said, "It sounds crazy but if you want it, then do it."

Not everybody thought my idea was great but no one ever doubted it was Lora Lee's kitchen and it worked like I thought it would. Everyone who came to the back door was taken in by the ceiling. The milkman looked straight up while he wrote down my order. One of the maintenance people from the college said, "We don't do things like this in New England—but we like it!" I don't know if he meant it or not, but like all the other guests, he couldn't ignore it. The covering was beautiful and when we more than quadrupled the ceiling light, the kitchen became a shaft of happiness on the darkest, loneliest days. Most of all, it was mine and I loved it.

But I have another idea about back doors and kitchens and places like that. The kitchen was my turf and I felt at ease—in fact, I felt I had the right to give a Christian witness to anyone who came to see me via the rear entrance. My approach focused on a pair of tawdry salt and pepper shakers I might have discarded in the move. They were the dimestore type I got at a Christmas exchange along with a grease container wrapped in the same package. That unattractive salt and pepper shaker set came from the lower end of the value line in a Sunday school class party exchange in a depressed year. The couple who brought the pair of tin shakers and the grease cup were naive new Christians who had never been to a Christmas exchange before, so they

**Every woman needs to do something to make her kitchen uniquely her own.**

signed a gift card while the rest of us discarded our white elephants anonymously.

But nothing I received that entire Christmas season thrilled me more than those tin salt and pepper shakers. The people who gave them had been alcoholics, crude family antagonists, filled with bitterness, and with no place in their hearts for church or religion. Their highest values were liquor, sex, and money. They had learned to live without God, but their system was reaping consequences instead of dividends.

Their visit to our church, which was the result of a solicitous invitation from a worried relative, became the life-changing event of their lives. At the end of the morning message Les gave his usual invitation for prayer at the altar and they came forward without hesitation.

What happened to them that morning bore the fruits of a radical change in both attitude and life-style. I know it doesn't work that way with lots of people, but they were delivered from alcoholism in an instant at the altar. And they have never turned back. In time he became an usher and she sang in the choir. Eventually, the church elected him to the church board where he served with sensitivity and compassion, showing none of the usual flare for authority so common among church board types. They sent their children to a Christian college. And, as for themselves they became beautiful trophies of grace.

This is why I wouldn't swap their cheap salt and pepper shakers for a sterling pair. And furthermore, the sterling shakers would never make a good opener for a Christian witness to some neighbor who came through the back door of our house for a cup of friendly coffee.

But there is one more reason why the back door is important to me. This is where I developed an early-morning ministry to neighborhood children.

Our boys were still in primary school when we lived in a parsonage with a small sturdy porch we had built at the back door. For reasons I do not remember, I began having prayer with Rich and Rog as the three of us stood together just outside the door on the porch. It seemed like it would have been better to pray inside because it was often raining. But we didn't. Perhaps we had an unarticulated desire to escape the clutter of the breakfast dishes or to change the smells of bacon grease for the crystal clean air off Lake Washington. Whatever the reason, we got into the habit of praying on the porch by the back door. Then after prayer I would hug and kiss each boy before they bounded down the steps and off to school.

Without realizing it was happening, I suddenly became aware of other children arriving early enough to get in on the prayer and the hug. Then for a long time I had a porch full of uninvited children who joined my hug line and joined in a quiet moment of prayer. Somehow, the word had gotten around.

"Lord, bless these kids today. Give them a good time at school. Help them to do their best in their work. Help their teachers to love them and understand them. Give special help to any child who is having a bad time at home. And be present, O God, with each boy and girl all day long. In Christ's holy name we pray. Amen!" Even the Supreme Court could not object to a prayer like that.

I love the back door. This is where we carry the groceries in and the garbage out—where the boys go to and fro with their friends. It is the unofficial family entrance. But in a special way it's my entrance to our house.

# The Red Carpet Out Front

WE'VE talked a lot now about the back door and the kitchen it serves, even its ministry. But the front entrance is no mean thing, either. There are many ways to help a doorway say welcome. I have used large coach lamps to soften the severe lines of an unornamented front wall, only slightly broken by a nearly flush door. I have hung baskets of bright flowers on the door or in the doorway and then changed them with the seasons. Since we have never lived in the sun belt, I am always rushing spring by filling the baskets or urns with tulips or miscellaneous spring flowers while stubborn banks of receding snow are still resisting the first hospitable temperatures of the new year. A burnished brass nameplate also has a welcoming effect on strangers who may be comforted by another opportunity to practice saying your name while they are waiting for the door to open.

However, the most effective welcome I ever built into the design of the front entrance was the installation of a red carpet from the public sidewalk up the steps to the door. I have always known the red carpet is the highest symbol of hospitality and honor. It is rolled out for visiting dignitaries in Washington. United Airlines maintains a Red Carpet Room for frequent travelers to major airports. The Peabody Hotel in Memphis rolls out a red carpet for the world's most pampered ducks who walk from the elevator along the carpet to the hotel pool each morning and back again each evening as stunned guests watch and cheer. The newspaper came out to photograph a twelve-foot width of red carpet Les had installed from the curb to the front door of our church. So— why shouldn't I have a red carpet entrance to our house?

This idea of a red indoor-outdoor carpet was new to the neighborhood, even the community. It was no easy matter to find a supplier who could furnish the right width and length

**Chapter Three**

**I had run red carpet from the sidewalk to the front door.**

and it was even harder to find a carpet layer who was willing to put it down after the maintenance people prepared the concrete surface. But with the support of my husband, it got done and the result was stunning. Pock marks, cracks, and broken pieces of concrete were now repaired and covered in an arresting red.

The red carpet was more than a conversation piece. For a time it caused near-wrecks on our corner. People slammed on their brakes without warning as necks craned toward our house. One evening, soon after the red carpet installation was complete, I heard a car stop in front of our house. Glancing out the window I saw a big long Cadillac out front that I was pretty sure did not belong to any of the faculty. I opened the screen door to welcome a noble-looking lady who was obviously concerned over something.

"May I ask you a question?" she said without a greeting, making no effort to walk through the door I held open.

"Certainly," I said, using my body language to keep suggesting she step in.

It was soon obvious why she stood outside the door on the red carpet. She wanted to talk about it. "What is this carpet doing on these steps?"

"Oh," I said, "This is the president's home and this carpet is to make the entrance look as nice as it can."

But she kept on pushing her query. "I understand that," she said, "but what does it do?"

"Do?" I replied, my tone reflecting a small frustration over what she was trying to get at.

"Yes," she said, "Does it keep the snow off?"

"No, I don't think so!" By now I was having patronizing thoughts. I couldn't understand why she couldn't understand.

Then she pushed again, "Does it keep the steps from wearing out?"

"No. I'm sure it doesn't."

The stately woman looked at the carpet and then at me and then at the carpet, repeating the sequence in a continuous motion. Then shaking her head, she courteously thanked me for talking with her and turned to go, saying, "I've lived in this neighborhood forty years and I've never seen anything like this before." And she left. She didn't ask me my name and she didn't tell me hers. My encounter with her was a social loss. I never saw her again. But for hundreds of guests and many more hundreds of visitors, the red carpet became a symbol of the warm welcome people anticipated when they came over to our house.

But the red carpet, bright flowers, coach lights, brass nameplate, or common welcome mat are only the first step in warming the atmosphere for visitors at your house or mine. Once inside, the social tempo changes. Outside it's the situation; inside it's the people. Here are some guidelines that have helped me to learn to be at ease as a hostess:

*One: If I'm at ease, they're at ease.*

Nothing is more disconcerting to guests than a hostess who is hyper, uptight, and tense. Murphy's Law says, "If anything can go wrong, it will." That is not true for the gracious hostess. With adequate planning and a modicum of last-minute attention to a good checklist, nothing needs to go wrong at all.

But, if something does go wrong by circumstances beyond our control, nothing will upset the guests unless it upsets the hostess. If she is irritated, overwhelmed, or frustrated over some irregularity, then the guests will be, too. They usually give her reassurances on why it doesn't matter, while she keeps showing her inability to cope by generating visible irritation. This sets up a counterproductive cycle that focuses all the attention away from the guests to the distraught hostess. When the evening mercifully ends, the people go home with a negative memory.

A relaxed, gracious hostess focuses on her guests who are more important than the salad that was left in the refrigerator or the charcoal that wouldn't light. People entertain people. Food, weather, and the serving processes are incidental to being together. It's the people who count.

*Two: Talk about things your guests enjoy talking about.*

Probing questions on sensitive subjects and far-ranging discussions on the personal weaknesses and inconsistencies of people not present are subjects that are off limits in Christian fellowship. Open-ended questions that contain such phrases as, "How do you feel about . . . ?" or, "What do you think about . . . ?" tend to give people an opportunity to express themselves as they choose. "Twenty questions" on any given subject tend to put people on the defensive. Yes-and-no questions tend to force people to take stands they often do not want to take.

Les and I have clarified some thoughts on conversations with friends and strangers in our house or theirs. (1) After 11:00 P.M., the conversation is likely to disintegrate and will probably become gossipy. (2) Whatever you say about anybody will sooner or later get back to them—distorted. There are no secrets; some things are just slower getting out. (3) A spiritual tone in a conversation is likely to be remembered and appreciated more than all the anecdotes and jokes you can tell. (4) It's always good to close an evening with a moment of prayer.

*Three: Never allow an embarrassing situation to develop over how you or they are dressed.*

We've all heard stories about people who went to a party thinking it was a formal affair and, as it turned out, they were the only ones in white tie and tails. That's the absurd case, but the formal or informal character of an evening needs to be communicated somehow in advance. Don't let your guests come dressed for a cookout if you plan a formal dinner by candlelight. Maybe I'm making too much of it, but I know some sensitivity is needed unless you do all your entertaining at Sunday dinner when people are dressed in their best.

*Four: Food does not need to be expensive to be good.*

A tureen of soup with heated crackers and a small salad can be very tasty, refreshing, and appropriate. The tureen itself can be a lovely centerpiece. The salad and the condiments can make a very colorful table. Great variety is possible in a menu that features soup and salad. Chili, oyster stew, clam chowder, and a long list of good soups are available with only small preparation needed for serving. The salad can be tossed, gelled, or waldorfed, made with spinach, lettuce, fruit, and fruit juices. Salads can have as much variety as you have imagination.

For the heftier eaters, dessert can be heavy. Pie a la mode, any one of a variety of cakes, or a personalized ice-cream sundae can be great clinchers to a very satisfying lunch at either noon-time or in the late evening.

Other inexpensive menu items include spaghetti with your option of tomato or meat sauce. Add a tossed salad and hot garlic bread and the meal is something to remember. Hot spiced grape juice can be a memorable starter. One good thing about a spaghetti dinner is its adaptability to wonderful decorations. Plaid table cloths and napkins can be bought or borrowed. They are available in both cloth and paper. Lanterns make good lighting. Baskets are excellent for serving the bread wrapped in a napkin that matches the table cloth. Fruit, if it is in season, can be a good dessert.

Another less expensive entrée for a very tasty meal is chicken a la king served in or on an open crust. Garnish the plate with slices of crab apple and add further color to the plate by serving frozen peas. They are bright green and they taste good.

I don't know why, but chicken a la king always calls for a red molded salad enriched with fruit juice, and a chocolate sundae for dessert. I suggest a fruit shrub if you need a starter.

Another less expensive dinner menu includes a good-quality meat loaf baked in a mold with a hollow center. Fill the center of the mold with peas just before serving. It can be both decorative and tasty.

Some of these, or none of these menus may meet your needs. But this one thing I know: expensive food is not essential to stylish, beautiful, well-received hostessing.

# Your Book of Memories

**Chapter Four**

ALTHOUGH one American family in four moves each year, we are not without roots. Only a few people stay for a lifetime in the home in which they are born. And few married couples live out their lives together in the house they first bought after their wedding. But this does not matter. We have other ways of keeping our roots deep. It helps to take our household furnishings from one place to another. The pictures on the wall, living room furniture, and dining room table service look much the same in one house or another. Nearly all of us have home movies, 35 mm slide collections, or scrap books. And with today's easy transportation, we often go back to the previous home or to the place where we were raised.

But there is another way to deepen and strengthen our roots that is most effective, and that is our family bank of memories. We remember the trip to the Falls, or the day Johnny broke his leg, or the time we were frightened by the burglar who turned out to be an extended limb of the old elm tree rubbing against the front porch. All these family happenings make great memories, but I have another kind in mind that has to do with those memories we have made on purpose because we planned a big event together. Somehow it got through to Les and me in the early years of our marriage that we could do something about enriching our lifetime together by generating some marvelous memories we could share with ourselves and our children for the rest of our days. It was out of this idea that we borrowed the money and made our first trip to England for Christmas. The journey had the overtones of a Charles Dickens Christmas. We walked over the cobblestones in the snow to have a midday meal at "Ye Olde Cheshire Cheese," which was frequented by Samuel Johnson and possibly visited by John Wesley. The last time it was rebuilt was in 1667. We held hands and looked up at the "The

Old Curiosity Shop," which looked liked it came right out of a Dickens novel. We went to St. Paul's Cathedral on Christmas Eve and walked along the narrow streets to a westend hotel where we were greeted at the entrance to the dining room by the sight of a roasted pig with a large red apple in his mouth. Then on Christmas Day we went to hear Dr. Leslie Weatherhead preach, an unforgettable experience. And that night, we rode across London in a little black cab to Westminster Chapel to hear Dr. Martin Lloyd Jones preach for an hour on why Jesus was born "to destroy the works of the devil." In the cab on our way to the service, Les and I had both made our conjectures on how many people would be present for the service. I said, "One hundred," but he said Dr. Jones was a famous preacher and there would probably be two hundred people in the service. Actually there were sixteen hundred people that night, every seat taken both upstairs and down. We really did not spend much money on the trip and we soon absorbed the cost. But we came home with a significant additional investment in our bank of memories that has added to our mutual enjoyment for all these years.

We make deposits in our bank of memories in another way and this is through reminders of special events and experiences. Somewhere in my personal memorabilia is a white straw hat with a tassel in the center of its top. It is an ordinary hat with an extraordinary memory attached. Les came home from the office one day to announce that he had been invited to go as a speaker with a contingent of college students who were being sent by our denomination on a mission to England and Europe. He said he was going to accept. I wanted to go with him. It was one of those situations in which I felt as though I couldn't, but I did. Traveling with college students is not without its burdens. And more than that, Les was going to be preaching two and three times a day in the public meetings scheduled for the group. Besides that, I had small boys at home and I could always rationalize that they needed me.

With the trip came a happy little memory I have always cherished. Before we ever left America, we were invited for tea in the office of the Lord Mayor in Bristol, England. I was told in advance that it was appropriate for me to wear a hat on this occasion if I wanted to be proper. I bought a white straw tam with a tassel on its side. It was very stylish and I was really proud of it. However, when I arrived at the office of the Lord Mayor for tea, I was surprised when one of the servants offered to relieve me of my hat, suggesting that I would be more comfortable if I were not wearing it. Surrendering the tam, I turned to the serious business of enjoying tea served on china with silver accouterments like I had never seen before in all my life, and all under a magnificent portrait of Queen Elizabeth. After we had visited for some time, the Lord Mayor suggested the students might like to be dismissed and that my husband and I visit with him for a few moments.

Perhaps we had visited longer than I thought, for then I looked out the window and saw the students in the village green playing frisbee. That was fine until it was suddenly apparent to me that the frisbee they were using had a tassel on it. It was my white straw, the hat on which I had indulged so much pride. It was a silly moment, and not worth the trifle to tell it again here, but it left me with a memory I cherish. You see, it does not take a big deposit to substantially increase my bank of memories.

But the most thrilling and important memories I have are related to people and situations represented by furnishings in our home. Let me tell you about just one: On the wall between the kitchen and dining room in our home hangs an exquisite Japanese art piece. It is a painting of a tiger on silk, framed with gold damask; high quality and—I am told—expensive. But it is not the commercial value of this work that makes it important to me; it is the memory it furnishes. One Sunday as I was shaking hands at the door of our church, I met a beautiful Japanese girl dressed in her kimono. She bowed and smiled but could not speak English. Her serviceman husband explained to me that Jitsuwei had come directly to Portland from Japan and this was her first experience in an American church. Across the weeks and months of that fall, Jitsuwei continued to accompany her husband to our services, bowing and smiling, but only able to understand what he explained to her.

Later that fall, Dr. William Eckle, a missionary of many decades of service in Japan, came for a missionary convention to our church. We told him how much we had struggled and how fully we had failed in trying to communicate the story of salvation to Jitsuwei. Although Jitsuwei was not a believer, her husband explained that she "feels something here."

Knowing the missionary speaker was fluent in Japanese, we were pleased and excited when Jitsuwei and her husband invited us to their home for a typical Japanese dinner. En route to their place, Dr. Eckle asked me, "Where is your gift?" I responded to his question with a blank stare saying, "We don't usually take gifts to people's houses when we go for a meal."

But Dr. Eckle said, "It would be a serious breech of etiquette if you were to arrive at this Japanese home without a suitable gift for the hostess." Under his direction, we located a lovely potted plant that was gift wrapped and carried it with us to the front door. While we waited for dinner, we enjoyed the sound of Japanese music that uses the pentatonic scale and sounded strange to our unaccustomed ears. But like everything else in a Japanese home, it was light, delicate, and unobtrusive. We sat on the floor for the dinner, which was as beautiful to see as it was to taste. But at the end of the meal I realized how much easier it was to get down than to get up.

I enjoyed everything, even the raw fish that we dipped in uncooked egg. Each dish was like a picture. I noticed that the hostess did not eat with us and asked Dr. Eckle why. He said, "Of course not. The hostess is part of the decoration for the meal."

At the end of the meal, Les and I noticed that Dr. Eckle was talking more seriously with Jitsuwei. Finally he said to us, "Jitsuwei would like to pray. She wants to accept Christ as her Savior." As he prayed in Japanese, I could not understand what was being said, but like Jitsuwei in our church, I could "feel something here." When she raised her head, her pretty eyes had beautiful tears coming out of the corners. The look on her face was shining and I could tell that something wonderful had happened as God gave Jitsuwei a new heart and a new spirit. Not long after that, she was baptized in our church, still in her native kimono. The cultural barriers had been no stronger than the power of Christ's love.

Almost immediately, Jitsuwei wanted to tell her father, a wealthy hotel owner in Tokyo, about her conversion and acceptance of Christ as Lord of her life. By her customs, she said this was necessary in showing her respect for him. He, along with all the rest of the members of her household, were Buddhists.

When Jitsuwei left Portland for Tokyo to tell her father about her conversion to Christ, the whole church was deeply concerned. We all wondered what his reaction might be. Our anxieties motivated prayers for her in every public meeting while she was away. However, when she returned to the United States, she brought the beautiful Japanese art piece that we have kept lovingly on our wall ever since. She said it came from her father who wanted the minister to know that he was happy about the conversion of his daughter and wanted to express gratitude for anything that made her more happy.

I look at that piece of artwork and although it is lovely, I think of a beautiful Japanese-American housewife who is serving the same Lord I serve and I realize no national customs can separate us from God's love. That painting of the tiger is a part of my growing bank of memories.

# Ease in Entertaining

*Be not forgetful to entertain strangers:*
*For thereby some have entertained*
*angels unawares.*
                    *—Hebrews 13:2*

# *Hospitality with a Christian Purpose*

## Chapter Five

*I* AM amazed at how much the ministry of hospitality is mentioned in the Bible. Some time ago at a Christian College Coalition dinner, Elizabeth Dole, who was serving in the president's cabinet, devoted her entire speech to college presidents and their wives to the story of Esther who had come to the kingdom for such a time as that. Esther's entire strategy for saving the Jewish people and retaining their freedom of worship was built around her ability to be persuasive across a luncheon table. She was a hostess with a religious purpose, and it paid off dramatically.

When Abraham was visited by the angels en route to Sodom, he negotiated a deal that moved from a flat-out destruction of the city to a willingness, finally, to save the town if only ten faithful people could be found. Abraham negotiated this dramatic arrangement with angels over a dinner served by his wife under the spreading arms of a big oak tree. The Bible even records the menu, which consisted of lamb, buttermilk, and cornbread. Not a bad lunch for angels!

The most important symbolic event in Jewish history is not the Dead Sea crossing or the ten plagues, but the Passover feast. Elijah, another great hero of the Jews, performed one of his greatest miracles to provide cornmeal and cooking oil for a poor widow and her son.

In the New Testament, food and entertainment are all the more prominent. Lydia is famous as a business woman who was a dealer in a very expensive purple dye. But she knew how to combine a career with homemaking, for she housed and provided meals for Paul and his three companions when they visited the city of Philippi.

Paul's son in the gospel was Timothy, but the sonship was apparently born out of the Christian fellowship hosted by

Lois and her mother, Eunice. The strong Christian relationship of father and son between Paul and Timothy was probably fostered more in the home than on the platform.

The ministry of Jesus was highlighted by many big events related to food and drink. The first miracle he ever performed resulted in 150 gallons of wine to save the newlyweds and the parents the embarrassment of running short on refreshments at the wedding reception. And those who were present at the wedding feast reported that the quality of the new supply of refreshment was significantly upgraded by the touch of the Master's hand. Jesus celebrated Levi's decision for discipleship by staging a big dinner for his unconverted friends. At least once, and maybe several times more, Jesus miraculously fed thousands of people. If you've ever tried to serve a tasty lunch to a huge crowd, you have some idea of what he was up against, even after the problem of ample supplies was solved. There is a sense in which the gospel era began with the Lord's Supper, which was a candlelight meal in an upper room in Jerusalem, and it will end some day with the Marriage Supper of the Lamb, to be served in the great expanses of heaven somewhere in the Revelator's city foursquare.

But for most of us hostesses who deal with the mundane matters of menus, shopping lists, cleaning, food preparations, and caring for ourselves, the story with which we easily identify is the hostessing of Jesus by Martha and Mary.

Jesus was a house guest of Martha and Mary during the last week of his ministry. He spent most of his days in Jerusalem, but he came home to their house each evening. Martha was the chef. She kept the cooking process on schedule and came up with everything ready, hot, and seasoned properly at the right time. Mary was responsible for her share of the work. She was probably supposed to set the table, help in a subordinate way in the cooking procedures, and then be a full partner in the cleanup. But she preferred talking with Jesus to any of these things. And this reluctance to serve and clean up irritated her sister Martha.

This built-in stress between the dynamics of entertaining and the element of fellowship leads me to the concept of hospitality with a Christian purpose. When you come over to my house, I have failed as a hostess if our agenda is limited to food, television, and games. There are so many ways to bridge the gap between the secular use of our home and making it hospitality with a Christian purpose.

Les's sermons were almost always practical in their application to Christian living, although he laced his messages with the strong chords of his theological beliefs. One of these sermons in a series on the home got through to a couple in our church. They decided to do some entertaining with a Christian purpose. She came to me with an offer designed to gladden the heart of any pastor's wife who is trying to do more than her time and energy will allow.

Catching me in the foyer of the church, she said, "Lora

Lee, your husband's sermons and the Lord have been getting through to me."

At first I started to comment on whether there was any connection between the sermons and the voice of the Lord. It sounded like she was separating the sermon from what God had to say. But I decided to keep still and let her keep talking. Although she was jocular in the way she expressed herself, I could tell she had something serious to say.

"We have a nice home for which we are grateful even though we worked hard to get it, and we want to use it for the Lord and the church and for you and Dr. Parrott."

I started to interrupt again because everything she said evoked a response in me, but I stifled the gush of words that wanted to come out from within me and substituted a smile and a nod in their place, shifting my weight from one high heel to the other. Eventually I got the story: She and her husband wanted to open their home to Les and me for our unrestricted use after church on one Sunday evening a month. All she wanted from me was the number coming. She did the shopping, preparations, and cleanup. All Les and I had to do was get out the invitations. She even insisted that Les and I stand by the door to greet the people as though it were our own home, and then bid them good night as they left. We saw immediately that this was going to be hospitality with a Christian purpose and we wanted to make the most of it.

We decided to invite all the new members or prospective new members in the church, along with certain people from the church board and their spouses. The hour or so we enjoyed together usually began with introductions, including a few words of background on each couple. Then three board members made brief statements designed to help our new people understand our church better. The information we dispensed was usually focused on where our people lived, the scope of needs being addressed by formal and informal responses in the church, our philosophy of church music, and other specific information on how our church functioned. Then we enjoyed lots of visiting with our refreshments. Over a period of years, we followed this same format with hundreds of new people participating. But each Sunday night, just before we closed the evening, Les gave a brief devotional word and had prayer with everyone. At first we were afraid to have a devotional since the people had already heard two sermons from him that same day, but we gave it a try and it worked. The devotional moments—never more than five minutes—were a real spiritual clincher to hospitality with a Christian purpose.

I know another woman who had a different kind of hospitality with a Christian purpose. Years ago when Les and I went to Toronto for meetings in Chuck Templton's Avenue Road Church, he took us to a large old home in an upper-middle-class neighborhood. Like most other houses in Toronto it was brick, but unlike most other houses it was large and built in a grand style with a huge porch across the front. At the door the pastor presented us to a sweet-spirited woman with a kind face, who made us feel like we were special people the moment we stepped across her threshold.

We soon learned that Mrs. Willis had put her house and her hospitality at the disposal of the pastor for entertaining church guests. She pampered her guests by serving tea in the afternoon and by bringing coffee and juice to the bedside for a morning waker-upper. Her breakfasts were always tasty and included hot scones with butter and jam. The other meals were arranged outside the home. The roster of names in her guest book read like a Who's Who of the evangelical world. Before we left, we came to see ourselves as honored people to be the recipients of Mrs. Willis's hospitality with a Christian purpose.

Many less dramatic ways can be found to plan hospitality with a Christian purpose. F. W. Boreham, the famous writer and pastor in New Zealand and Australia, had an Englishman's sense of privacy and reserve that made it difficult for him to confront people openly with the gospel as though he were a religious salesperson. To bridge the gap between his reticence and their needs, he wrote personal notes to people to whom he felt impressed to write. He spoke briefly of his concern for them and suggested his availability to meet with them personally. If he got a favorable response, Dr. Boreham took the initiative in setting up a time and place for fellowship with a Christian purpose. And through the years, he won hundreds of people to Christ with this strategy of hospitality.

Some women have their own version of Christian diplomacy. Since Dr. Boreham spurned both the telephone and the automobile, his letters and notes were about the only options he had as individual means to the heart of a person with spiritual needs. Most women I know are good on the telephone and can push without pressing. They can tell when to pull back or move ahead in setting up a luncheon date or a coffee break. Restaurants are good places for spiritual rendezvous. The only better place is your home. A private coffee klatch or a personal lunch with someone who is hurting is probably most effective in the home—that is, if you feel comfortable using your house and your social graces for this purpose. If so, you are practicing hospitality with a Christian purpose.

# Keep It Simple

esus did the impossible when he fed five thousand men, not counting the thousands of additional women and children who walked in the shadows of their Mideastern husbands and fathers. The total crowd may have been ten thousand or even twelve thousand or more. They were not organized into neat subgroups that could be easily directed. They must have been tired families and parts of families who by now were irritable as most people are who are hungry and see no prospects of food. Added to the sights and feelings of hungry adults were children and babies who wailed and contorted in the desert heat, from which they had no escape. Food, shelter, and water were all one big mirage—the projection of false hopes.

To the disciples, the people and the situation must have looked like a huge crowd does after the breakup of an outdoor concert, or the milling of thousands on the beach when word is out that all food stands have no supplies and the water fountains are dry. The disciples expressed a low-level concern for the people but soon dismissed their responsibility by declaring the situation impossible. Even if there were enough food, which there was not, what about all the other needs for serving. Who brought the styrofoam cups, where were the paper plates stored, and who could take hold of this situation and get everyone seated and a set of orderly procedures underway? If they ever fed this kind of huge megacrowd, the leftover refuse would be strewn across the desert for miles. This might result in a court citation from the Romans. And everybody wanted to stay out of the way of the Romans. In a conquered country they were bad news.

But the one person who could turn all this social chaos into joy was Jesus. He performed the miracle that was more than the orderly production of food. He organized the seemingly

**Food does not have to be expensive to be good.**

unmanageable horde of men, women, and children into workable groups of fifties and one hundreds. He schooled the disciples in how to serve—not only with an efficient hand but with a loving heart. And when the meal time was over there was not a wrapper, a flying napkin, or an uneaten sandwich on the ground. The place was litter free and all the leftover food that is always a part of entertaining was neatly stacked away in twelve baskets. Truly this was a miracle.

Jesus doing the impossible by feeding the multitude is a miracle every hostess can understand. When I first started my ministry of hospitality, my biggest fear was failure. I was afraid of omitting something important. I've always been haunted with the idea of leaving the salad in the refrigerator. (I did that once.) And once I didn't think about the relishes until we were eating our dessert. I had worked on them for an hour making roses of radishes and curlicues of carrots. Then there was fear of some key ingredient being left out of a recipe or too much salt added to the broth, or a cake that fell in the oven. I had fears about whether I would look all right, whether the guests would actually come, and whether they would have a good time if they did. It was awful. I wanted to entertain well. I read all the helps I could get on how to be a good hostess. But I didn't know how to pull everything together at once and make my hostessing a dream instead of a nightmare.

**Simple is better than elaborate.**

Then I decided to count on a miracle. I would plan, prepare, work hard, and keep a good attitude, but I knew a lot of things were beyond my conscious control. I decided to stop worrying and stewing, to enjoy being a hostess and to make my home my ministry. What the Lord did in the miracle of his hospitality has much to say to us women today if we are going to learn the ease of entertaining.

*One: Simple is better than elaborate.*

I learned from Jesus' serving miracle that simple food is more appropriate and easier to work with than elaborate dishes and fancy menus. I have often wondered how Jesus served all those thousands without styrofoam or plastic. I know the commentaries have their answers but I also have mine. I wonder if he could have used pita bread or pocket bread, which would have held a meat serving of flaked fish or a handful of small smelt-like fish. This was the simplest of menus but it provided a tasty high-protein serving of fish in a land where bread was considered the staff of life. It was like hamburgers on a bun in our day, or fried chicken and french fries, or a steak and baked potato. Simple is better than elaborate.

*Two: Expectations are more important than expertise.*

Every country in the world has its own food norms. Within each country are regions with their own flair for food. Canton and Shanghai both produce fine Chinese dishes but they are quite different. In America there are definite regional differences in eating habits that are quite distinguishable. Southern cornbread made from stone-ground white meal is not to be confused with northern johnny cake even if they look very much alike. Chicken or shrimp gumbo from New Orleans is not to be confused with New England clam chowder, nor even New York's Long Island version.

People in big cities are more cosmopolitan in their tastes for food than people in rural America. In a country that must have had its exotic foods, Jesus performed his miracle with the kind of food a boy would carry in his lunch.

Knowing what people expect is more important than proving my culinary expertise in preparing something that doesn't suit their tastes. I saw once what happened to my succulent gourmet dish—most of it came back to the kitchen sink on the plates. Thus, I learned another lesson from Jesus' miracle of hospitality and committed myself to serving what the tastes of the people have come to appreciate. Thereby I have saved myself the agony of being a fancy cook. I have learned that expectations are more important than proving my expertise on a dish my guests have trouble appreciating.

### Three: Tranquility beats agitation.

One of the lingering lessons that got through to me from Jesus' serving miracle was the power of being quietly self-possessed. A flurry of human agitation is never a proper prelude to service. Jesus surveyed the scope of the need, calmly sought out the small resources that were available, clearly instructed his helpers on what they were supposed to do, had prayer, and went about the business of multiplying his resources. I've thought about the times I got agitated and then overwhelmed and frustrated my own purposes by letting my emotions get unsettled and my mind addled. I decided hostessing like that wasn't worth it. I've learned that my best serving events come when I'm self-possessed, in charge of myself, and in charge of the situation. It makes entertaining easier. Tranquility beats agitation.

### Four: People want to help.

There was a time I tried to do it all, but not anymore. By looking at the relationships of Jesus and his disciples, I learned that you can find a dozen people to help you, if you take true lead, who would never attempt the project by themselves. It's the decisions and the willingness to start slicing the first loaf that overwhelms most of us. What will we serve? How will the people be seated? How do you want this bread cut? Who is going to clean up? These are the kinds of questions that helpers ask. If you have the answers, they're usually willing to work. The disciples were willing to take on delegated responsibility as long as Jesus held on to central authority. And that division of labor still remains—responsibility and authority—in the biggest and best serving events of our lives. People do want to help. All they need is motivation, instruction, and the kind of job they can handle without getting too deeply involved.

*Five: You're never through until you're through.*

The story of Jesus' serving thousands would never be complete without the twelve basketfuls left over. The second piece of pie or another round of sandwiches is social insurance against embarrassment. Not every family who ran short on refreshments at wedding receptions was fortunate enough to have Mary in the house to call on her son Jesus for help in saving the situation. For me, it is better to have leftovers than to run short.

*Six: Keep your own record.*

The ease of entertaining is increased by keeping your own record of the event. I use a large bound ledger-type book in which I make several notes after each social event in my home or for ones that are my responsibility in the church or on the campus. This includes names of the guests, menu, decorations, and any special information such as what I wore, since I keep my clothes a long time and don't want the same guests having to see me in the same thing every time they come to my house. Even if it doesn't matter to them it does to me.

*Seven: Let the memory linger on.*

William Barclay, in his Daily Study Bible series, said he wanted three things to happen when he went to church: something to think about, something to feel, and something to do. I would add a fourth happening in Christian hospitality—something to remember. I am sure that contrast in hunger and satisfaction and all the overtones of the miracle of bread and fish made the people remember their dinner on the grounds for all time to come. I am sure children passed the story on to their children and grandchildren, saying, "I was there." Not all, but many of our hostessing events need something left that says, "I was there." The memory needs to linger. A small personal gift, a name card, a long-stemmed rose for the women, a little book, or a recipe card are some of the kinds of mementos with staying power. Unless it becomes expensive, a photograph of each couple at some important event is a wonderful way to keep the memory of it alive.

*Eight: A spiritual presence.*

Years ago I made a decision that every social event in our house would include some kind of spiritual presence. Les and I try to make saying grace more than a ritual by setting up the moment in prayer with a line or two about gratitude or love and concern for each other. We have a grand piano in our home that is put to good use to accompany a song. If the situation seems appropriate to the idea, someone is asked in advance to be prepared for a very brief devotional word and a prayer. This comes at the point in the evening when it is apparent that everything is about to break up. But regardless of how or when, every social event needs a spiritual presence.

*Nine: No situations are impossible.*

For years I have kept my own loaves and fishes in a special place in the cabinet for the unexpected guest. To frozen bread and canned tuna I have added some tasty soups, quality preserved fruits, and perhaps, ice cream. It's not much, but it has turned many a situation into a happy event when it might have seemed impossible. My freezer is a treasure chest of good things waiting for the right happening.

So there you are. The story of Jesus' miracle of feeding the multitudes is full of suggestions and thoughts for the Christian hostess who is committed to being good at her craft by putting ease into her entertainment.

# Unconditional Hospitality Is Not the Answer

## Chapter Seven

AT certain times in my life, hospitality has not always been the answer to the situation. The first time I saw that hospitality was not unconditional was at 9:00 on a Sunday morning, forty-five minutes before time for Sunday school. Although we lived next door to the church, the final forty or fifty minutes before any church activity was always a mosiac of uncoordinated movement, trying to get my two little boys—one preschool and the other nursery school age—and myself ready for worshiping God in public. Nine o'clock on any morning was their finest hour and on Sunday they were at their best at practicing passive resistance while I tried to dress them. I had put the older boy in a chair to one side and told him not to move while I laced up the younger's white hightop shoes. I was on my knees in front of him in his little red chair working intently on the laces and trying to keep his hands out of my hairdo when the doorbell rang.

Threatening them both if they followed me, I dashed down the steps to the front door thinking it was a flower delivery or an emergency message. Then through the glass I saw a tall, thin, widow with a severe hairdo who felt a strong need for some psychological closeness to the pastor. Except for her big smile she could have posed for Grant Wood's painting "American Gothic"—that's the one with the farmer holding a pitchfork standing by his daughter in front of a rural church with a gothic motif. I was stuck. She saw me and obviously I had seen her. But I still took hope. Maybe she was just dropping by with some little gift for the pastor's family, like a jar of jam or a pumpkin pie.

I opened the door, and as soon as I said, "Hello!" with a cheery upturn of my voice, I realized my worst intuitions were true. She had come to visit.

"I got here early—and since there is no one much in the

church yet, I thought I'd just come over and spend the time visiting with you."

I forced a weak smile and said, "Sit down." If she had been more sensitive she would have felt the emotional sag in my voice. I gave her a copy of *Reader's Digest* to read and excused myself to go back upstairs and finish getting the boys ready. Their half-dressed condition was apparent from the top rungs of the stairway, where they had ventured to see the visitor. They looked like prisoners in a jail for cherub angels as they stared down through the bars at her and me.

As I turned toward the stairs the boys scampered back to their places as though by doing it I never would have known they had moved. But I wouldn't have scolded them anyhow because I was preoccupied trying to decide how to handle the situation downstairs. I realized I was not dealing with hospitality; I was dealing with a precedent. If I encouraged someone who was insensitive to my problems as a young mother living next door to the church, she would come back again and probably again and again teaching other insensitive people to do the same.

I made a decision: I would wait her out. My gift was hospitality but it was not without its limits. I closed the bedroom door quietly, finished dressing the boys, repaired my hairdo once more, and then sat down between the boys and read them stories until a half hour later I heard the front door open and close. It was the end of the matter. She never came back to visit right at church time. I was glad for Les's sake that there were no seeming ramifications. I guess she found other ways to meet her need for privilege or psychological closeness to the pastor's family. But I learned a strong negative lesson from the experience: Unconditional hospitality is not always the answer to other people's needs.

I learned something else about unconditional hospitality in a left-handed way from a single girl who was the best I have ever seen in trying to make her problems ours. Her usual method of operation was to drop by unannounced at our house on Sunday nights after church. Already exhausted after multiple services, Sunday school, prayer meetings, practices, informal unofficial meetings, and all the other things that make Sunday a twelve-hour working day, her uninvited presence at our table was beginning to irk Les and me more and more. I knew how I felt and I could tell how his emotional temperature was rising as his answers to her became more crisp and his prayers more pointed. But Les was the one to do something about it. He loved Sunday in spite of the horrendous work load. It was his favorite day of the week even when it rained. I actually think the time after church on Sunday night was his most relaxed and reflective hour of the week. He always said he felt more like eating and laughing after church on Sunday nights than any other time all week. And now this girl was ruining it all by coming for professional help at an inopportune time. She sat at our table and poured out an hour of self-expression all focused on her self-pity. For the privilege of listening to this emotional indulgence we shared our Sunday night supper and disrupted a private time that had priority with us.

The woman kept on coming several Sunday nights a month. We began to realize she was becoming dependent on us to fill a lonely vacuum within her that the usual social opportunities did not afford. She was too old to be with the teen-agers, and being unmarried she was self-conscious about couples gatherings, so she turned toward us. All of this was fine, but not on Sunday nights after church.

We had just said grace and were starting to enjoy our meal when the doorbell rang on the Sunday night that changed her life. We both knew without looking who was there.

Les said, "You go ahead and enjoy the chowder while it's hot and I'll talk with her."

Within ten minutes he was back at the table. She was gone and I was reheating his clam chowder and warming the crackers.

"What did you say to her," I asked incredulously. "You must have made her mad."

"Oh no," he said, leaving the table to stand in the doorway to the kitchen. "She might get mad and if she does we'll have to deal with the fallout when the time comes. But I just tried to help her see that the cure for her loneliness and self-pity was not to become increasingly dependent on us, but to find some way to shift the focus of her concern from herself and her bruises to other people and their hurts and concerns. That's pretty straight medicine and she may not take it."

For reasons we will never fully understand, the shy, easily hurt, socially inept single girl decided to use her time going home each day from her job at the telephone office to visit people—cold turkey, house to house—and invite them to our church. As she kept to her plan of visitation, her personality began to change. Her fearful ways gave over to an increasing social confidence. People liked her and began responding to her invitation. She became a fixture on the front steps of our church in good weather and inside the big doors in bad, where she waited to greet her friends. Later I learned she used two hours each Saturday to visit rural people.

Not only did her personality change, but her life. She developed scores of friends and one day one of the young men she met proposed to her. Today they have a lovely family. The change took time—months, even years. In fact, it is still going on. But the motivation for it came out of a brief conversation that helped me understand that hospitality is not unconditional under all circumstances. There is a time to put your foot down. Letting people run over you doesn't make them good drivers.

There is one other kind of person who does not need our unconditional hospitality: the nosey neighbor. Les and I had one neighbor directly across the street from us who was

**Letting people run over you doesn't make them good drivers.**

omnipresent—to use a good theological word—behind the curtains of her front window. Sometimes we saw the curtain move and sometimes we saw her. But even if we didn't see her we always waved because we knew she was there. She had been on the lookout for our predecessors and she was doing us the same favor. One way we knew about her breakfast-to-bedtime watch was the consistent reports we got back on our comings and goings and who our visitors were from the circle of people she contacted regularly on the telephone.

It really didn't matter. Her watching us did not break our bones and most of her telephone reports that logged our activities were harmless, gossipy chit chat. But one day, after some years, we got fed up, not with the nosey woman as much as with the people in the congregation who enjoyed being on her line. We decided to play a joke on everyone.

After lunch on a Wednesday we made a big show of packing the car with our suitcases and driving off after we waved good-bye to the moving curtain in the front room of the house across the street. We didn't go far, however. We got the boys and ourselves ice-cream cones at a shop several blocks away and then returned home. We did not turn into the drive as usual, but parked the car on the other side of the church, around the corner, and left the empty suitcases in the trunk. Then, we slipped into the back door of the parsonage. When we showed up for the midweek service that night, there were surprised people in the congregation, particularly the ones who had been told by those on the line that the pastor and his family had left on a big trip and nobody knew where they had gone. After that, it was never again quite as much fun to get the nosey neighbor's reports on the comings and goings of the pastor. Nothing was ever said and the woman did not stop watching us; it just wasn't as much fun.

**Les and I had one neighbor directly across the street from us who was omnipresent—to use a good theological word—behind the curtains of her front window.**

# When Everything Goes Wrong

THERE have been a few times when everything has gone wrong and my best efforts to be a gracious hostess have ended in failure. In fact, one of my most humiliating memories comes from an evening when I tried my hardest to have dinner for some very distinguished guests. Les had invited a key leader of our denomination to preach a series of messages in our church. We had always admired him and his wife from a distance, but now we were going to have them in our home for dinner. He was a kind man with a sense of humor, but he did not smile very much and always talked with a sonorous voice that made me feel uncertain and sometimes inadequate in his presence.

He and his wife, who also was going to be with him for the series, were world travelers. They had eaten in the finest restaurants on most of the continents and had been guests in homes in which superior cooks had entertained them with flawless elegance. I was just sure of all of this when I started to make my plans and choose a menu I thought would be especially impressive to them.

I attempted dishes I would ordinarily have avoided, but I was eager to do a fine job hostessing this distinguished visitor and his wife. Right after lunch I set the table with our best china and personally went to the florist to choose a centerpiece of roses to match the candles I had already bought. And even if I do say so, the table was beautiful.

All afternoon I had continued along the critical time path necessary to bring everything up at the same moment for a delightful dinner, cold dishes cold and hot dishes hot. I reminded myself of the time Les and I were invited to the breakfast table in a home in which the proceedings were interrupted after we sat down by ten minutes of family devotions that allowed the eggs to get cold, the bacon grease to

**Chapter Eight**

congeal, and the toast to get clammy. I had chuckled at the thought and recalled my mild resentment toward the hostess who did not know how and when to get things done. But as for me and my house, we were going to have an elegant dinner on time with everything just right.

I had just turned my attention to the makings of a crisp green salad, when suddenly it all happened. For reasons unknown, a disposal which had worked perfectly for many thousands of times, suddenly malfunctioned most dreadfully and backed up horrible-looking black murky water into the sink. I mumbled something to myself about keeping cool and that this was no time to panic as I reached under the sink to push the reset button. But there was only horrifying silence broken by the rumbling of the black water as it continued to rise in the sink ever higher. I pushed the button again, hopeful for some kind of a grinding, buzzing sound. But, alas, there was utter silence.

Still mumbling aphorisms about quietness of spirit, I took a firm hold on the long wooden salad spoon and thrust it into the dark hole of the disposal where I shook it vigorously hoping it might loosen whatever was jammed and let the water flow through. Deciding the time had passed for calm self-assurance, I panicked, crying at the top of my voice, "Les, come here this minute . . . something terrible has happened!" He was downstairs straightening up the books on his study shelf so that they would look just right for our esteemed guest.

Sailing up the steps, two at a time, he came charging into the kitchen and took in the whole situation with one big exclamation, "Oh my goodness! What are you going to do?"

Mercifully, the water stopped backing up, but it made no indications whatsoever of any intentions to recede. It settled in like the black waters of a murky lagoon after a big storm. It was there and there to stay. After a quick conference, we decided to call the best self-educated, unlicensed plumber we had in the congregation. Fortunately for us, he did not live far away and was soon at our place with all of his muddy hoses, some long links of a metal device he called a snake, and all sorts of wrenches and mallets. Seeing his pick-up truck loaded with all of this assortment of stuff did not fully reassure me, but it was comforting.

His opening shot to me as he stood over the sink was not necessarily enlightening. He said, "Your disposal is stuck." I already knew this, but maybe there was some value in two of us having the same diagnosis.

My home-study plumber went to work with a vengeance. What he lacked in knowledge, he made up in aggressiveness, and, unlike some professional plumbers on big hourly rates, he had brought all of his tools with him. I sized up the situation very quickly and knew that, what I saw was what I was going to get, and I had better hope he was lucky.

The first thing he did was to cut off the electricity in the entire house. I am not sure why he did this, but I do know it caused havoc to the oven dishes and stopped all of my progress on the stove-top cooking procedures. Moments later, he had his muddy garden hoses strung out across our front yard, up the steps, over the railing, and through the kitchen window. We looked like the last stop on the road to desperation. Although it was not raining, he had on rubber boots which tracked his mud back and forth through the house and across my kitchen floor. I could have cried for the time I had spent on my hands and knees making those tiles sparkle.

I wish there were a happy ending to this story, but there is not. While he was still working at the kitchen window, I happened to see him waving to somebody outside and horror-struck, I realized that my distinguished guest and his wife had arrived, all of our efforts to locate them in advance and cancel the dinner having failed.

They were gracious, loving people and insisted that we not desert our plans for eating at home in favor of a restaurant where, he said, he had to eat so many of his meals. But I served him oven dishes that were undercooked, potatoes that were not quite done, and vegetables that still had most of their original color. By now the disposal was working and the voluntary plumber was gone. But the meal was in shambles, and I was fighting to hold back the tears. Our guests were using every reassuring approach they had in their public-relations kit to make me feel at ease, but frankly, it didn't help much.

I have never had the nerve to invite that man and his wife back for another home-cooked meal. I imagine they chuckle whenever they see my name on a cookbook. I only have one ground of comfort to stand on and that is the fact that his wife told me about her own experience of failure. I am confident that every woman who reads this story will identify and respond with some kind of a tale about her time when everything went wrong.

Perhaps it is like locking the house after a burglary or closing the barn door after the horses have run away, but for whatever it is worth, here are some suggestions on what to do when everything goes wrong:

*First: Laugh.*

I would tell you to cry but I know from experience that it does not help. Once I was serving a dinner on the lawn at our home by the river. We had either miscalculated the number coming or ten people had shown up who were not invited. Suddenly, I was surrounded in the kitchen by so many people giving me instructions on what to do to save the moment that I rejected all of them emotionally and burst into tears. Then Les had to take over and, with the help of the caterer, divided some serving portions to stretch the food over the increased number. It would have been a lot better if I could have laughed at myself. Instead I took it all too seriously and was embarrassed after everyone went home.

*Second: Do something.*

Some problems in life have no solutions and our only option is to adjust. Unfortunately, some things are just beyond our control. But when it comes to entertaining, some kind of positive solution can almost always be found to nearly every problem. In the great number of official and unofficial dinners I have hosted as a college president's wife, there is one couple Les and I have invited to join us more often than any other. We have two or three reasons for why we like to include them in the group. For one thing, they help to carry the conversation. Second, they have a sense of the appropriateness of the situation. Third, they always know how to help rescue me out of a tough problem when it is necessary. If there is excess noise, uncertain results in the kitchen, slowness in the service to the table, or any other of a long list of hosting problems, they don't just sit there; they do something.

*Third: Be at ease.*

The title of this section is Ease in Entertaining. This does not mean that entertaining is easy, but it does mean that the hostess can be at ease in her entertaining regardless of the situation. No problem will be any bigger than the hostess allows it to be. The undercooked roast or the melted ice cream will only damage the event to the extent that the hostess allows it. Laugh a lot. Don't just stand there; do something. But most of all, be self-possessed if you want ease in your entertaining.

# The Silver Punch Bowl and French Iced Coffee

## Chapter Nine

THERE is only one recipe in my collection that I have kept secret. It has never appeared in any of my cookbooks. I have never talked about it to womens groups or even shared it with my closest friends. But I probably have served it to more people at college receptions, dinner parties, and special events than any other punch. And that is the reason, of course, for trying to keep it secret. I want it to be a treat when people come to a campus event at our home or wherever.

As a compiler of cookbooks, it has sometimes been difficult to say no, but until now the recipe for French Iced Coffee has been unpublished.

Usually, the conversations among the curious follow a line like this:

"I'm sure there is ice cream in it."

"It has coffee ice cream in it, no doubt."

"I wonder if it has whipped cream?"

"I'll bet there's ginger ale in it."

This kind of talk makes me feel guilty because ordinarily I share all I have or know. But for years I've withstood the pressure and just kept on filling the silver punch cups with French iced coffee from my silver punch bowl.

During receptions someone is sure to say, "I don't like coffee," but everyone says this is really not like coffee. Sometimes teen-agers drink so much of it their stomachs hurt after they go to bed.

All my recipes are not this successful, I can assure you. But this one, which was given to me by a West Coast friend, Mary Anderson, is probably my all-time prize.

The punch is good enough on its own, but it helps it to be served in the silver bowl and matching cups given us by our

**Until now the recipe for French Iced Coffee has been unpublished.**

59

congregation at the celebration of our twenty-fifth wedding anniversary.

Guilt feelings when serving French iced coffee are one thing. When writing about it, the bad feelings get stronger. I have had people tell me they have experimented in many different ways to concoct this special punch. I am sorry for all the ingredients used improperly. No, it does not contain ice cream! Here is the treasured formula:

### French Iced Coffee

*3 cups strong coffee*
*2 cups sugar*
*1 pint cream or half-and-half*
*1 quart milk*
*2 tsp. vanilla*

Dissolve sugar in hot coffee. Cool.
Add other ingredients. Pour into milk cartons to freeze.
Remove from freezer 2 hours before serving.
Mix and serve very icy.

I feel as though a secret pal has just been revealed! Enjoy!

The French iced coffee is not the only recipe I put in the special punch bowl. Another favorite is frozen banana-pineapple punch. This has been submitted for many cookbooks. It is a good one and especially pretty in the spring time. To me it is a little filling and not as refreshing as some punch recipes. Makes about 18 punch cups.

### Banana-Pineapple Frozen Punch

*5 bananas, blended or mashed*
*2 large cans frozen orange juice (12 oz. each)*
*2 large cans frozen lemonade (12 oz. each)*
*1 large can pineapple juice (46 oz.)*
*4 cups sugar*
*6 cups water*

Mix together and freeze.

Take out of freezer two hours before serving and add 2 quarts of ginger ale. Makes about 50 punch cups.

An appetizer for the Christmas holidays is frothy and pretty. My blender is not large enough to handle more than enough for twelve dinner guests, although I think it would be beautiful in the punch bowl. Here is the recipe:

## Cranberry Froth Appetizer

Combine cranberry juice and good quality vanilla ice cream in a blender to the consistency of a thick milk-shake. Serves 12

The lovely pink color starts any dinner with a festive mood.

Many times my entertaining includes groups too large to serve the costly French iced coffee and the banana-pineapple recipe. I am always searching for something different and less expensive. The tired old Hawaiian Punch and ginger ale route was just not exciting enough.

The answer came at a retreat in the Ozark Mountains. The women in charge had big plastic buckets of a frozen punch and served a huge crowd. I use the recipe often and always at the annual reception for seniors and their families in the month of May.

## Frozen Ozark Punch

*4 small or two large packages gelatin (3 or 6 oz. each)*
   *Lemon or any other flavor can be used.**
*5 cups boiling water*
*6 cups sugar*
*8 cups cold water*
*16-oz. bottle lemon juice*
*2 bottles pineapple juice (46 oz. each)*
*3 large bottles cold ginger ale, about 1 quart each*

Dissolve gelatin in boiling water. Add sugar; mix well. Add cold water. Let cool. When cool, add lemon juice and pine-apple juice. Mix well and pour into plastic containers tightly covered. Freeze. When ready to use, dip container in hot water to loosen. Place in punch bowl. Add ginger ale. Punch will be slushy and will need no ice. Makes about 75 punch cups (add more ginger ale if short).

Punch should be removed from freezer the morning it is to be used and placed in refrigerator.

---

*I use lemon gelatin in the above recipe to represent the gold of our purple and gold school colors. At Valentine events, strawberry or raspberry is used. This is one recipe that can blend with any color scheme.

A good standby, this punch has an amusing name.

## PTA Punch

*1 large can pineapple juice (46 oz.)*
*1 large can grapefruit juice (46 oz.)*
*2 cans frozen orange juice, thawed (12 oz. each)*
*3 bottles ginger ale (28 oz. each)*
Mix together and serve. Makes about 50 punch cups.

The following recipe is a favorite. Students have told me that when it is in the freezer, they enjoy it frozen with no thawing whatsoever. And it is best when snitched and consumed all by itself.

## Fruit Slush

*1 small can orange juice concentrate (6 oz.)*
*1 small can pink lemonade (6 oz.)*
*1 small jar maraschino cherries*
*1 large can crushed pineapple (15 oz.)*
*1 pkg. frozen, sliced strawberries (15 oz.)*
*4 cups water*
*1½ cups sugar*
*4 bananas, sliced*
Mix together and freeze. Stir as mixture starts to freeze.

# Pleasure in Raising the Children

*When I was a child, I spake as a child,*
*I understood as a child, I thought as a child:*
*But when I became a man, I put away*
*childish things.*
*—1 Corinthians 13:11*

# Boys and Stairsteps

## Chapter Ten

THERE is a time for babies to be born. I am not talking about the gestation period following the miracle of life when the parts of the human body are completed for delivery, but rather, I am speaking of the time in our lives when we are emotionally ready to share ourselves with a permanent new member of the family. For Les and me this time came nearly nine years after we were first married. When we left college, we had a lot of growing and developing to do within ourselves. During our college years, Les's father was president of the institution and my dad was a leading trustee. It had been a stressful time because the college was moved from a small community to the advantages of a larger campus in a thriving little city a hundred miles away. It is a principle of life that resistance to change always comes from vested interests, and in this case the property owners and those with long emotional attachments to the old location had used their full strength in trying to block the move and discredit its leadership. Les felt this pressure keenly and believed that many persons thought it was safer to take out their frustration on him than it was on his dad. Then in our junior year, a disruptive bombshell caused my father to change denominations and resulted in deep confusion and hurt lodged far within the joint psyche of our natures. Having each other was a saving factor, but it did not alleviate the confusion in our minds.

Our solution was radical. We went to the local Sears store and bought a little one-wheeled trailer that we attached to the back of our Plymouth coupe. With all our earthly belongings in the trunk of the car and piled onto the trailer, we started for the farthest place away from home we knew about, which was the Pacific Northwest. It would not have been any more radical than moving to New Zealand or Australia would be today. We wanted to go to a place where no one knew either of us or had any experience with his dad, the college, or my parents. I am glad we did not have children during this time because we had lots of spiritual learning and changing to undergo. Les was enrolled in graduate work in Willamette University and I owned three candy concessions in department stores in Salem, Albany, and Roseburg that provided the major income for our support. Outwardly, we were doing fine, but inwardly we were still torn apart. We had moved to a new country, but we had brought our old problems with us. Our minds were still tortured with the memories of things we could not understand and by people who by our standards, contradicted everything they proclaimed in their faith. We almost despaired of our souls.

One saving factor was the good church we had found and the kind, godly pastor we were fortunate enough to have. It had been several years now since we left college, but all of our growing had been academic or financial, not spiritual. I still feel it was a good thing we did not have babies during this time in our lives.

However, our church had an old-fashioned revival meeting that we attended regularly. We liked the evangelist and we knew it pleased our pastor for us to attend. On a Monday night, for some reason, we sat forward on the right-hand side, the very first couple in the congregation. I am sure the evangelist preached a good message, but he did not give an invitation, it being Monday night and with an afterglow still present from the great services on Sunday. But it would not have mattered, because Les and I never had let it enter our minds that *we* had a problem. It was all of *those* people who had done wrong who needed to straighten up and fly right.

However, after the service was over, something very unusual and life-transforming happened to Les. We went back to the little two-room attic apartment where we lived near the university. It was an upper level that had been reclaimed as a rental to graduate students. Les says that people who have done this to graduate students are going to be held accountable in a special way at the final Judgment. But maybe it is not as bad as he thinks because they did provide us with low-rent space within walking distance of his classes and my candy business. But there in the bedroom of that little apartment, Les got down on his knees by the side of the bed and began reading the Bible, praying, and talking about our spiritual predicament. It was finally in spiritual desperation that he said, "If there is no one in the world who is sanctified, I still believe this experience is taught in the New Testament and I want to possess this kind of spirit. I can't go on like I am."

That night something wonderful happened to him which I could perceive immediately. He even looked different. Somehow he had been able to take all of the past with its problems, people, and self-inflicted punishments, and put them as a package into the hands of God. There was without a doubt a new spirit within him. I had the same kind of life-changing experience some ten days later. For the first time in our lives, we felt as though we were ready to live with each other and for something beyond ourselves. It was really the beginning of the great life-long experience we have enjoyed together.

For one year, Les became Dean of Students at Northwest Nazarene College and I became society editor for the Nampa Free Press. But at the end of that year, the second great step occurred in our lives that put us on the track, which has led us through many a beautiful hill and dale together. We left the college and the newspaper for Les to become a pastor in Kelso, Washington. We sold the candy businesses and told the Lord we would leave the money-making enterprise to the laypeople he had called to that ministry while we gave ourselves to pastoring the church. What God had begun on our knees in the little two-room apartment near Willamette University, was now completed in our immersion in a ministry of pastoral concern. We were happy beyond bounds. The old attitudes and old ways of thinking were behind us. We loved each other and we loved our church.

We were on the top side of our middle twenties and we both knew without hesitation that the time had come for us to have a baby. Having a baby was a part of our spiritual growth and the next step in the development of our love for each other. Nine months later I was lying on a bed in the maternity section of the old hospital in Longview, Washington. The hospital, which used to be the railroad station, had been made into a beautiful facility. It was the greatest moment of my life. I was propped about with pillows and surrounded by my husband, the attending physician, and a smiling nurse who had just placed our son, Richard, into my arms for the first time.

Later that day, I had the baby in my arms again, alone this time with no one to distract my thoughts. Alone, just him and me, I began talking to him. I told Richard how long we had been waiting for him and how the time for his arrival was just right. I told him how he was the most important thing in our lives. Once my words began to come, they flowed easily and finally hummed along like a purring sound as I beamed all over myself, talking to this marvelous little person God had helped us to create. I told him all about the church and the people who were waiting to receive him into their love, how his father was a preacher, and how the people who listened to our daily broadcast each morning had been writing letters and sending little gifts as expressions of their love toward him. I told him about the Kiwanis Club which held a special shower for his dad in preparation for the coming of the baby.

Then I told him how I wanted to be a good mother, how I did not know much about babies, and how my younger sister had always been the unofficial, but fully-employed babysitter in our neighborhood. But lest he have any fear, I assured him

**It was the greatest moment of my life.**

we would get along just fine. I had already talked at great lengths with my mother and she had given me some advice that I found out was the best I heard from anybody who tried to help me learn how to care for a new baby. She said, "Lora Lee, just take one day at a time."

Finally, in the privacy of that white room that used to be part of the railroad station before it became the hospital, I said, "Richard, I'm going to pray with you right now." I held him close and prayed and thanked the Lord that the waiting time was over and at last my baby was in my arms. Then I continued to pray and I asked the Lord to bless our lives together. I asked God to be with him as he grew to be a happy, healthy young man. I prayed he would give his heart to Jesus when he was old enough to understand. And I prayed that the Lord would use his life to the fullest of his purpose. I will always feel that the baby smiled at me when I said a soft, "Amen."

It is no wonder that two of the places we love to visit in the Northwest include the little two-room apartment near the campus of Willamette University and the old hospital in Longview that had been converted from a railroad station. We were two very fortunate young people because God had given us our first child at the time when we were ready to receive him.

Each of us takes our babies when God gives them to us, but it is wonderful to feel that we have had fair time to plan for their coming. This is the way it was with the second boy in our stairsteps of sons. It was less than a year after the first boy was born that we were swept off our feet by an invitation to become pastors of a larger church in a far removed part of the United States. We had lived at the foot of snowcapped Mount St. Helens where Spirit Lake was the trout fishing place for Les and lots of other men in our valley. Our freezer was filled with supplies of beautiful pink salmon and luscious fruit that is typical of that area. It rained a lot but everything was beautiful and the winters were mild. Les was writing a weekly column for the newspaper and most of the people in our valley knew us from our 7:00 A.M. broadcast five days a week. And with a new baby, we could not have been happier.

But apparently in God's purposes, the next phase of our lives was at hand and we were ready to exchange all of the plus factors of the Pacific Northwest for an opportunity to serve a divided church in a highly industrialized city, unionized to the hilt, and in a state known for its long, severe winters. But that was all right, too. Without even talking about it, Les and I knew that sooner or later we were going to go back to the country where we grew up and where we had gone to college. The grace of God had redirected our attitudes and we were ready for the next phase in our lives. We stayed in Michigan eight years to the Sunday.

Not long after Les and I arrived in Flint, we began to lie awake nights talking about when the time was right for a second baby. It would be easier to raise one child at a time, but it might be better for both children if they were nearer the same age and had each other as companions and protectors during their growing-up years. I had already heard horror stories about what happens to mothers with two babies in diapers. But we finally came to the conclusion that two babies could not take any more time than one since the only child occupied all of our time and energy anyhow. The decision was made. We would have a second child as soon as possible, we hoped while the first baby was still very young.

And the next June, the second stairstep in our family was filled with the arrival of a very healthy baby we named Roger. He was born in a better hospital, but with no better start in life than his brother, twenty months older than himself. Unfortunately, the new baby had trouble with his formula and we never did seem to get it right. He suffered from chronic colic that kept us up with him night after night. There were times when we got so tired we actually took five minute turns in walking the floor with him.

I remember one time when I was exhausted beyond my capacity to endure. It was early in the morning and I had gone through another sleepless night. Not hearing any car come into the driveway or any sounds on the front porch, I was surprised when the doorbell rang. I went to the door half resentful, wondering who would dare to come so early in the morning. But I burst out with a shout of glee when I looked through the glass and saw my mother standing on the other side of the door. How she knew when to come is more than I can understand. But maybe this is the way it is with God and mothers.

With the coming of the second son, we had a lot more to learn than how to buy diapers in large quantities and where the baby formula could be secured most reliably. We thought it was the greatest idea in the world to have two boys near the same age to look after each other. But we had not taken into account a new term Les learned in his classes at Michigan State University where he was by now working on his doctoral degree. At three, four, and five years of age we were having problems with the boys. And we could not understand why. The boys were dressed alike and most people thought they were twins. This made us very proud, but the fact was they did not get on with each other, and the older one particularly had a nasty attitude toward me that could be ignited by nearly anything I did for the younger one.

This was about the time Les came home from the university talking about a conversation he had had with a clinical psychologist friend of his who had taken time at lunch in the cafeteria to explain the meaning of sibling rivalry. Children in the same family, he said, are afraid there will not be enough love from mom and dad to cover all their needs. Therefore, they compete with each for the favor and love of their parents. Now is the time, he said, to stop dressing the boys alike and stop trying to treat them as though they were identical when in fact they were not. The psychologist told Les to recognize that each boy had a different personality and each one was to be encouraged to be himself or the boys would grow up to be bitter, angry adults.

It was strong medicine for a young couple who thought they were already being ideal parents. But we took the prescription and started the long process of helping each boy to be fulfilled in his own right as a person who could count on unconditional love and acceptance from both mom and dad without interference or complications from his brother. That is a mouthful just to write down on a sheet of paper, but it was even much more overwhelming to practice as we started restructuring our relationships with the boys and their relationships with each other.

From further study, we learned that the oldest son is typically more self-righteous than the younger, that he is usually more dependable and will work harder to secure the love and trust of dad and mother. We learned that the second son is usually the clown in the family. Unable as a baby to match strengths with an older brother, he will oil his way smoothly through family circumstances by being winsome and funny. He tends to disarm his opposition with his charm and his jokes. But we also learned that the second child, as in the Bible story, is usually the prodigal. He gets sick and tired of the righteous ways of his older brother, who always gets the immediate approval of mom and dad, who trust him with the money and with the most-important assignments. And in the presence of the second son, the parents often lecture the older son about his responsibility in looking after his younger brother when the two of them are away from home. Fed up and fagged out, the younger child is more likely to leave the family and go into the far country where the family values are rejected and replaced with those that stand in strong opposition to the priorities of mom and dad. In fact, the best way in the world for a prodigal to strike back at mom and dad is to flaunt his rejection of all their values and priorities.

We did not learn these lessons easily and they had to be relearned from time to time. Our older son was good in his studies and so the younger one decided to major in athletics and not in textbooks. At one point, his passive resistance expressed itself in an unwillingness to learn how to spell. Les or I would drill him on his words on a Thursday evening until he could spell each one of them beautifully, but then he would come home on Friday after school with a test paper indicating he had missed half of them. We were beside ourselves until we learned again that what he needed was our unconditional acceptance, not our approval that came at the end of a successful experience in spelling class. It was great raising those two boys. In many ways they did complement each other and were great friends. But in a hundred other ways, they never failed to let us know that each one of them wanted to be a person in his own right without comparison with his brother, and most of all, each of them wanted our unconditional love.

We have always promised our boys that we would pay their tuition as long as they went to school until they got doctoral degrees, even if they were married. This has been a costly promise, and thus far two of them have cashed in on our commitment. But it was most interesting to us to observe that the second finished his doctorate when he was only twenty-five years of age, putting an academic fire under his older brother like you can't believe. Looking back, raising boys to be wholesome, mature, young adults has been a bigger challenge than my marriage. In marriage I have worked beside and loved a mature man who understood me. Often he played the supportive role in raising the boys because he has been away from home so much during the last dozen years of their growing up at home. But in raising children, the boys were unable by their immaturity to be a supporting member of the cast. They were totally dependent and most of the time I had to provide the understanding and maturity for both of them and myself. Frankly, there was not always enough to go around.

But there's one more boy on these stairsteps of sons. Two factors spelled out his fortunes as the third child in the family separated by some years from his older brothers. First of all, his older brothers would be his main tutors. But they loved him in an unpredictable way. I soon learned that the twin factors of cooperation and competition are seldom absent in any relationship in life, but especially in the relationship between older brothers and a third son.

Trying to help the older boys accept this new member of the family, Les took them and me for an expensive dinner in the main dining room of the Olympic Hotel in Seattle. It was a fancy place where they served some of the entrees on flaming swords. The waiters dressed like Egyptians with great turbans about their heads and flashing jewels shining in the subdued light of the dining room. Because the place and the event were important, I borrowed a fur coat from my mother, hoping to look more in keeping with the surroundings. But when one of the waiters complimented me on my coat, the younger son—remember, they always have the jokes—piped up and said, "Oh, it's not hers—she borrowed it from grandma."

That same second son had nicknamed the new baby "hon-abun" the first time he looked at him. The older boys were always good to Les III and he became a much better child than he might have ever been without them.

But a second important factor was in molding his life. He was the third child, the apple of his father's eye and a child who obviously wore a coat of many colors in the eyes of his older brothers. We tried not to let this happen. We had numbers of ways to equalize our love among the boys, but we could not escape the fact that he was the last child, that we were older now and more able to do things for him than we were for the other boys. Furthermore, he fully knew how to play his status to the hilt. He's newly married now and entering graduate school with his dad paying more expensive tuition bills than he ever thought of for the older boys. But as I look back at more than twenty-five years of raising boys, the three of them have more than tripled the joy in my life. They drained off the highest level of my energies, caused me most of my sleepless nights, and in return filled me with levels of satisfaction and happiness I never could have known if God had not given them to me. Many times they competed for the attention my husband actually needed and they won. And many times Les might have been different to me, but they were always there. It was hard to be alone even when we were alone. But on balance there is nothing in life that has been more fulfilling than my pleasure in raising three sons.

**It was hard to be alone even when we were alone.**

# A Cherished Moment in a Child's Faith

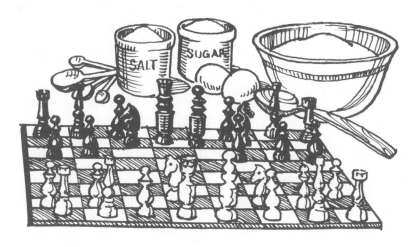

I T was a snowy day in Michigan: not a blizzard—just steady white snow coming down to make the earth beautiful and new. Les had gone to Detroit for a district meeting of some kind and it just seemed to me this was the right day to spend in my all-pink kitchen that was the most attractive feature of our brand-new parsonage. It was a treat for me to bake cookies, but I seldom had time. And now everything, including the elements, was just right for me to fill the house with the aroma of baked things.

I was up to my elbows in the mechanics of cooking when my two little boys, ages four and five, came into the kitchen from the family room, one of them holding the chess board and the other one carrying an inlaid box of chess pieces.

"Teach us how to play chess," they said, totally oblivious to what I was doing with the cookie dough.

They could hardly have made their request at a worst time. I was right in the middle of preparing a recipe that could not be dropped. My first maternal reaction was to tell them to wait until I had finished in the kitchen. But with the eagerness in their eyes and the warm feeling I had about the whole day, I decided to do two things at once, make cookies and teach the boys how to play chess. I am sure I was intrigued that such little men would be interested in the complex game of chess.

"Let's put your game here," I said as I pulled out a bread board. Sitting on two high kitchen stools, the boys listened intently to my instructions on how to place the chess pieces on the board. I grinned with pride as I saw how quickly they caught on to the names of the various pieces. And I was further pleased to see how fast they learned the limitations of each move, that the castle could only move vertically and horizontally, not on an angle, that the horse could move two

**Chapter Eleven**

spaces up or down and then one space to the right or left, and that the king could only move one space at a time.

In between guiding the moves of their game, I was stirring and mixing and adding ingredients. All of a sudden the oldest boy, with an awful look on his face said, "What's that?"

Unsure I said, "What do you mean—what's that?"

He continued to snarl his face as he said, "That terrible smell in that bottle."

When I held the bottle of vinegar close to him, he put his small hand over his nose and mouth, making gurgling sounds as a prelude to the big exclamation, "Take it away."

I said, "Richard, this is what they gave Jesus to drink when he was thirsty on the cross."

With sincere anguish coming from his eyes, he said, "Why would they do that?"

I stopped the baking process for the moment. Replacing the cap on the vinegar, and, turning away from the chess board, I said, "Let's go in the other room and talk about it."

As we walked out of the kitchen into the family room, Richard poured out a vial of naive, sincere questions like, "Who would do that . . . why would they do it . . . why didn't someone stop them?"

In the best way I could in the language of a five-year old, I explained how Jesus died on the cross that we might be forgiven of all our sins. I told him that Jesus could have fought back or could have accepted relief for his suffering, but he chose to die alone, just for us. I quoted the best-known verse in the Bible, "For God so loved the world that he gave his only begotten Son, that whosoever believeth in him should not perish but have everlasting life." Then I went back through the verse, inserting Richard's name to make it more personal and easier for a child to understand.

He listened without changing his expression and said when I finished, "I want Jesus to come into my heart and I want to tell him that I am sorry he was treated like that." By this time tears were running down his small cheeks. Together we slid off the davenport onto our knees and let the coffee table become our altar. We told Christ in our own way how sorry we were that he had been thirsty and they offered him vinegar. We told him that we knew it must have hurt when they pushed a crown of thorns on his head. And we said we could not imagine how anyone could put nails through his hands and feet or push a spear into his body.

By this time the second son had caught the spirit of what was happening and I heard his whispered prayer, "Jesus please come into my heart, too."

The simple faith of those little boys, four and five years old, shown through their tears and their smiles as they hugged their mother, both at the same time. We just sat quietly for a few moments and then went back to the kitchen where we picked up on the chess game and the preparation of the cookies.

It would be several weeks before the signs of spring would come—the robins, the daffodils, and warm sunshine—but that snowy day was Easter in our hearts on Mackin Road in Flint, Michigan. It was a cherished moment in the faith of a child and in my faith, too.

# Teaching the Bible to Children

## Chapter Twelve

LES loves to tell the story of his most exciting childhood day, the time his mother took him from Bethany into Oklahoma City to choose the Bible story book that she would use to teach him. With all of the options laid out on the floor of the store, he examined each one from the vantage point of his hands and knees. I am sure he chose the one with the brightest pictures and largest print, *Egermeier's Bible Story Book*. Day by day, over a period of more than a year, his mother interrupted the morning schedule to sit down and read him a Bible story. When she finished, she asked him to retell it to her. If he was not able to do this, then she would either read it to him again, tell it to him in her own words, or sometimes act out the story with him until she was sure he knew it.

From this experience, Les and I determined early on with our boys that the childhood years were the time for our children to learn the narrative content of the Bible. Just as children learn the basic tools of education—reading, writing, and arithmetic—during the first six grades, we believe they should learn the primary material of the Bible as given in the beautiful stories it contains.

We wanted our boys to learn the narrative content of the Bible while they were children. We had seen far too many children who were biblically illiterate.

About this time there was a popular book written called *Why Johnny Can't Read*. It assailed the new picture method of teaching boys and girls to read in place of the old approach of memorizing the ABCs and putting sounds together by uniting letters of the alphabet. In the new approach, dear to the hearts of liberal school administrators and seminar speakers, was the built-in idea that in due time a child who learned to read whole words at a time would also learn to understand

**I am sure he chose the book with the brightest pictures and the largest print—*Egermeier's Bible Story Book*.**

the letters. But Les, who was the head of the psychology department of George Fox College at this time, besides pastoring the church, said he could spot students who had come through the Scott Foresman method when they read in class because they often failed to put the final syllable on a word that distinguised it from present tense to past tense. For instance, they did not add the sound *ed* on the word *call*, and thus confused the present tense with the past tense. He said they were reading by word and not by syllable.

We reasoned that this kind of problem that was apparently nationwide in public schools, was also analogous to the problem of biblical illiteracy that we saw so many times. We decided to take the matter into our own hands with our boys. We would assume responsibility for teaching them Bible content at home.

The first thing we did was to make a list of the major Bible stories of the Old Testament and the New Testament. We identified the lives of the major characters that would need in-depth study. We identified passages of Scripture that we wanted them to locate easily along with other portions of the Bible that deserved memorization. It was a crude approach and I am sure it lacked sophistication, but it got us started.

One of the most effective ways we had of teaching Bible stories to the boys was to act them out. When they divided up the roles to be played in the story of Jonah and the whale, I think there was some symbolism in the fact that they wanted Les to be God and me to be the storm.

**I think there was some symbolism in the fact that they wanted Les to be God and me to be the storm.**

And now I have a grandson, Andrew. I have not checked matters lately, but I have a suspicion that very little has changed. If our children are going to master the narrative content of the Bible, I think the responsibility for this teaching will rest upon the home. The church does a fine job in teaching morality, standards of behavior, churchmanship, and church history. But when it comes to basic Bible knowledge for children, I believe this is the special province of mom and dad for each child.

If you decide that the teaching of the narrative content of the Bible is your responsibility, then here are some very helpful suggestions that may make the teaching-learning process more effective:

*First: Buy a good Bible storybook.*

Although every child needs a Bible, it is likely that their Bible storybook will be a more important tool in their process of learning the narratives. Go to the Christian bookstore and take enough time to analyze all of the volumes they have available. A Bible storybook is not good because it is old, or better because it is new. Do you want modern pictures or old-fashioned ones, lots of white space or closely printed words? Do you want the chatty, upbeat type of storytelling or the more traditional approach? If you take home Bible teaching seriously, your children will look back on the Bible storybook you used as one of the most important volumes their family ever owned. This decision is of utmost importance. Buy the right book.

*Second: Make Bible study important.*

The children will soon catch on to the importance you place on learning these Bible stories. They will believe it is important if they are convinced you think so, too. If you are haphazard in your approach, easily skipping days or full weekends, then the children get the idea that reading the Bible is something you do when there is nothing else more important to take its place. Do not start this kind of Bible study program with your children unless you intend to commit yourself to learning systematically. Work days, week days, holidays, holy days, and special days—all look alike from a child's prospective. It is what you do on any given day that makes that day important.

Choosing the time and place is also important in making Bible study a high priority for children. Studies in teaching and learning have strong emphasis on systematic use of the same time and place. After a few days of conditioning, the mind of the child is ready for learning the moment the time has come and they are in their usual place for learning. Educational psychologists believe time and space are important in learning.

*Third: Read well.*

In a day when our children have good quality educational television, there is no place for a teacher of Bible stories to read in an unattractive way. Even if you have to seek professional help from an acting teacher, learn how to take on the voices of the characters and read their lines with feeling. Children watching "Sesame Street" may learn by indirection, but boys and girls learning Bible stories will remember what is made to sound important and attractive. The quality of the reading is directly related to the ability of a child to remember.

*Fourth: Use teaching aids.*

Marvelous materials are now available for helping boys and girls learn the narrative content of the Bible. Your local Christian bookstore has an ample supply of these helps or can order them for you. One of the popular ways of teaching is through using attractive flannelgraphs. The Lutherans and Moody Bible Institute people have done an excellent job in developing filmstrips on Bible stories. There are a few 16-mm films on Bible characters, but for the most part, these are too expensive for home use. Perhaps you could get other families to join with you on rentals if these films seem important enough for the teaching of your children. But most of all, help the children learn to act out a Bible story. They will remember what they can visualize. Acting comes naturally to children. It is lots of fun and the children will never forget the experience. Your children will have as many good ideas on how to set up the story, assign roles, and put on the production as you will. If you have enough ambition, you can take on a summer project in the backyard of laying out the walls of the Old Testament temple or the geographical lines of Palestine. But maybe this is too much. We used to use the cities of our state to represent the places in the ancient world that were important in the story of the Bible. This gave the children during their junior high years a fairly good concept of space and distance around the Mediterranean.

*Fifth: Keep trying.*

Trying to teach the narrative content of the Bible to your children may be like taking three steps forward and two steps back. There were times when I felt as though we were making good progress and other times when I wondered if I was getting past the thinnest membrane on the surface of their young brains. But I got one reward that was never published and there is no way to hang it on the wall in the family room. When the boys enrolled in a Christian college, they were given a standardized test on Bible knowledge that was to be used in placing them in a required Bible course. Both of them ranked so high on the test score that the head of the religion and philosophy department came to Les and wanted to know how our boys had learned so much about the Bible at an early age. He told him what I tell you, "We just kept on trying . . . not very good sometimes . . . but we never quit."

# Building Family Traditions

## Chapter Thirteen

WHEN Les and I were first married, we got paid on Sunday night, cashed our check on Monday morning, and then apportioned out our resources for the week ahead. The first week we did this, we started some family traditions that have stayed with us for a long time. First, we took out our tithe and put it in a vase on top of the mantel. Then we put four dollars in a matching vase. This was enough to let us go out for a meal at a restaurant on the Sunday noon just before we were paid again—when we might not otherwise have any money left. Third, we took ten percent of our money to match the tithe and paid ourselves in a savings account. I could not believe how much we had saved by the end of that first year. It was hard at first, but after we got started and money began earning interest, the savings account became lots of fun. At one point, we changed the system by going to the bank the first week of each new calendar year to borrow money equal to what we thought we could save in a year. Then we would work hard to pay off the bank note by the Fourth of July.

Lots of traditions developed in the family as the years went by. But when it came to raising the children, there were some traditions that became so strong, no one in the family dared ignore or attack them:

*First: Never on Sunday.*

"Never on Sunday" became a catch phrase to cover a rule that was never broken at our house. On Sunday morning there was never to be anything unpleasant brought up in discussion or behavior before the family went to church. Even the children knew they would never be disciplined before church on Sundays. It might be raining or snow could cover the ground, but at our house on Sunday morning there was never a discouraging word. If Les and I had reason to disagree—and there were plenty of times when we did—it never happened on Sunday morning. We decided that preparing our own minds and hearts for going to church was as important as the service itself. Even if we got bad news on the telephone, it was tucked away and not brought out for amplification and discussion until after we got home from church. We thought it would be wonderful if we could have tranquility at our house all of the time. But this being impossible, we decided that the least we could do would be to dedicate the time before church on Sunday to quietness and positive reinforcement with each other. "Never on Sunday" became more than a tradition; it became a heart-warming blessing.

If any bad news was phoned in, I knew it could wait until after the morning service to be reported. Unpleasant messages are often phoned on Sunday morning because guilt and anxiety can overwhelm people during the unstructured hours of a weekend. People's hurts and hostilities will crescendo and explode on weekends because there's more time to think about them. But never on Sunday were these kinds of messages allowed to upset the atmosphere in our home before church. In one church Les had an arrangement with the treasurer not to talk with him until after church. Otherwise, the treasurer thoughtlessly dropped bad news on him just before he went into the pulpit.

As a corollary to this tradition, most of the preparations for Sunday were well under way and usually completed on Saturday. The rituals of Saturday included checking the children's clothes, getting hair cuts, taking baths, and polishing shoes. The white baby shoes were cleaned, shoe laces washed and put back in their eyelets, shirts pressed, buttons checked—all on Saturday—because it saved the unnecessary possibility of increasing tension on Sunday morning.

One thing that worked well at our house was the weekly Sara Lee coffee cake as a Sunday morning breakfast special. It was the only day we had this delicious treat. After the boys got older we needed two coffee cakes, and at one time I was buying three. Now that they are gone, I don't buy any, and I miss the ritual. It was just a nice little happy thing we enjoyed on Sundays.

In connection with this tradition, we learned that rushing did not enhance the spirit of Sunday morning. We usually set the clock for an hour earlier than we thought was necessary just to give us more time to be at ease. We learned to leave for the church in time to be early instead of on time. Samuel Johnson wrote in his journal about the "scheme of life for Sunday." He said, "Rise early and in order to do it, go to sleep early on Saturday night." Les once preached a sermon the people talked about for a long time, "How to Break the Sabbath on Saturday Night." A peaceful beginning to every day is desired, but a tranquil beginning on Sunday morning is a necessity at our house. You see, Sunday is the most important day in our week.

*Second: We can't fight their battles.*

This is a litigious age when there are more lawsuits, letters to the editor, protests, and threats and counter threats than ever before. The most natural thing in the world to do for our children is get out there and fight their battles. It's part of the parental psyche.

I always wanted to fight back because hurting my child was worse than hurting me. I am so deeply involved emotionally with my children and my husband that it would be easier for me to agonize myself than to watch anyone of them suffer. Those boys are a part of me. I am their mother. I'm inclined to feel it is not right for anybody ever to hurt them because they are mine. I know how wonderful they are and what their motivations must be and how any failure on their part should be understood and not used against them. But Les and I decided a long time ago that it was not only impossible for us to fight their battles, but running their interference was doing them a disservice. This does not mean that we would fail to help any of the boys in any kind of a situation whether or not they were guilty. But it does mean that we never focused blame on other people in a way that would make our child feel protected from the rules of life. Making a child feel he or she is exempt from the laws of life is counterproductive in helping him or her grow toward maturity. Overprotection only teaches the child that he or she is a special kind of person and that no one is ever to let him or her down. The overprotected child learns to expect perfection from everybody and to see the whole world occupied by fools who never do as they are supposed to do by the child's standards.

One dark, rainy night when Roger had been sent to the drugstore on an errand, he came charging back into the house through the kitchen door with tears bursting out of his eyes and his voice agitated. "I'm so mad! I'm so mad!" he screamed.

At first, all I could get from him was that he was mad. But after he lowered the decibels of his voice and his heartbeat had decreased some, he went on to say, "That crazy guy hit me on my bicycle and he didn't even care."

Our first response was to dash out the door, call the police, or do something dramatic because a hit-and-run driver had hurt our eleven-year-old boy. And as Rog said, "He didn't even care."

About that time we heard a knock at the front door and a nice man, himself visibly shaken, had come to check for sure that Roger was not hurt. We all calmed down together and everything worked out nicely. The man got the bicycle fixed, Roger was not hurt physically, and his pride was soon mended. I guess I am not against being belligerent toward those who have hurt my children, if I thought this would do any good. But I really feel deep down that trying to fight their battles beyond a certain minimal point teaches them a wrong set of nonproductive attitudes and sometimes leaves emotional scars that are worse than the original problem.

*Third: Disappointments are inevitable.*

Peter Drucker said that any person who gives himself or herself unreservedly to the corporation is defenseless before its inevitable disappointments. But disappointments, sometimes great and sometimes trivial, are a part of life. I wish it were possible to keep my children from ever being disappointed, but there are times when I have to let them down. Plans do change and situations develop that are not anticipated. Our boys, like all other children, would invariably try to heap guilt on me for the disappointments they suffered at my hands. But I had to learn and then teach them that disappointment is a part of the human predicament and there is no way we can escape it. Therefore, I cannot afford to feel guilty just because I have to disappoint my children.

I know of one mother who tried to save her daughter from disappointment to the point of visiting three beauty shops in one day. She said, "I have spent an enormous amount of money on her, but I just didn't want her to be let down over her hairdo." Unfortunately, the girl did not even like her hair after it was done the third time. The mother's time might have been better used in helping the daughter to deal with her disappointment by adjusting her emotions and working on the hairdo herself at home. Unfortunately, the daughter's demanding attitude toward her mother will be taken into her marriage some day where it will be expanded manyfold.

When cleaning and sorting a box of old school papers and books, I came across an essay written by one of our boys when he was thirteen years old. He does not indicate his hurt, only the problem. Here it is with the spelling corrected:

• • •

### My Trip That Never Was

About five months ago I was planning to go on a very exciting trip. I was planning to go to Hawaii with my dad. The trip was based on how well I did in school. My dad thought that might motivate me and since he had a speaking engagement down there, he would take me along.

I went through my whole first semester dreaming about the palm trees, the ocean, and everything that ever was near Hawaii. To say the least, my dad thought my grades were good enough for the trip to the islands.

It was the night before our trip. I had my suitcase packed, I had a list of people to send cards to, I was excused from school (for the next few days), and everything was great.

I was sound asleep until about four o'clock in the

morning. I heard a knock on my bedroom door. It was my mom. I was half awake and all she said was, "Dad is sick with the flu." I thought that I was dreaming.

I woke up only to find that my trip would not be a reality.

The End

•   •   •

I am sure the disappointment was great. For a child to have to tell the teacher and the kids, "I did not get to go," is not easy. The dreams of a far-off island had been in vain. And the chance to be with his dad did not materialize. The unpacking of the suitcase was not enjoyable and the stamps already purchased for picture postcards were put in the desk drawer for future use. I am not sure what we did, if anything, to help this boy work through his disappointment. I imagine he learned very soon that everything in life is a trade-off. I am sure that his dad substituted something just as exciting for a later experience. Another thing is certain: we cannot protect our children from disappointment.

*Fourth: Heroes of the Faith.*

Another great tradition at our house had to do with the attitudes we developed toward leaders in the church. Local congregations are made up of marvelous people who nevertheless sometimes have irksome ways and can on occasion be downright difficult. In almost every local congregation a few people can be found who seem to get their kicks out of complicating the existence of the pastor. Since our goal in raising the children was to help them internalize the values and priorities of the church we loved, we decided that they should never hear us speak unkindly or in a critical way concerning members of our congregation regardless of the provocations. This commitment was not always easy to keep, but it was kept. Also, we decided to let the children get well acquainted with the leaders of the congregation by holding church board meetings in our home. Halfway through the meeting, whenever Les gave me the signal, I would serve refreshments. We taught the children that this monthly meeting of the board in our home was a happy occasion. As much as was possible, we let them be the servers of the refreshments. On one occasion, they filled their little red wagon with bottles of Coca Cola and pieces of cake that they took around the circle to each member of the board. One child would pull the wagon and another would push, and both would serve. On one particular occasion, one of the boys came in the room to present a proposition on making a basketball goal post in the driveway. After stating his case, he sat there, listened to the discussion, and heard the unanimous vote of the board to move ahead on his project.

**One of the boys came to the board to present a proposition on making a basketball goalpost in the driveway.**

Another part of our tradition with the boys was to invite preachers and church administrators to our home for a meal when the children could be present at the table. On one occasion, I asked a denominational leader if he were willing to eat hamburgers and baked beans so that the boys did not think we always had expensive meals just when the important people came.

The first time I ever heard one of my sons outline his career plans was at the dinner table when he told a guest that he planned to be the most outstanding fund raiser he was capable of being. The church leader picked up on what he said and encouraged him fully, even reminding him to this day of their conversation back in his teen years.

I heard another one of our sons talking long distance some time ago to a Christian scholar in another state from whom he was seeking advice about his graduate program. He had heard that scholar preach, but he really came to know him at our dinner table.

I have had great pleasure in raising the children. Les has been on the road a lot, but I made a decision to stay home on purpose until the boys were in college. Now they are raised and looking back, I see that raising the children was divided into two phases. Until they were twelve to fourteen years of age, they needed me for their own survival. I was probably the most important person in their lives, alternately with their dad. But after fifteen years of age, as I look back on it, I only had the influence over the boys that I had earned. At an increasing momentum, they were more and more able to take care of themselves and they felt their need of me less and less. That is the way it should be. But that is not the way it is with mothers. I have had a big struggle letting go of the boys. I only wish they still needed me as they did before.

I try to be of help through endless suggestions and admonitions, but they smile wryly and usually look toward their father for the direction they need now. But that is all right, too. I feel as though we have reached our goals in raising the children. They are healthy and strong physically. Two of them have advanced degrees and the other one is working on his. Their marriages seem sound and strong. Most of all, they love our Christ and have given themselves fully to his church. I was not perfect and I am more aware than many others of the mistakes I made along the way. Perhaps it is in spite of me that they have turned out to be what they are. But no one can ever take from me the pleasure I have had in raising the children.

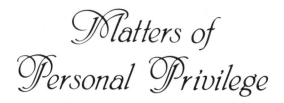

# Matters of
# Personal Privilege

*"Oh, how happy is the woman who believes
in God, For he does make his promises
to her come true!"*
*—Luke 1:45 (J. B. Phillips)*

# Unconditionally Me

YOU may ask any specialist, "When do you start to train a child?" and the answer will come ringing back, "Fifty years before he is born." By the time we can speak the language of the culture into which we are born, we are the victim of it. Our possibility of changing the culture is just about as great as a tiny baby has of getting the nonsensical syllables of his baby language accepted into the adult conversation. I know that a child born in Wilmore, Kentucky, and raised in Fort Wayne, Indiana, will have some kind of a special Midwest stamp that will never fully fade away. I could have been born and bred in southern California, or the state of Maine, or New Zealand, and then things would have been different. But I am from Indiana and I need not fight the fact that those Midwestern values closely related to the soil and the early development of the prairie country have found their way into my internal system. They are a part of me.

## Chapter Fourteen

I was born to a beautiful mother and a highly motivated father. Mother taught me about manners, clothes, and how to entertain. Dad taught me how to get things done.

I remember dad telling about a church he visited in Birmingham in which no one knew him. It was the last Sunday for the departing young pastor, who was being reassigned after the church's conference the following week. Dad listened to the young pastor give a full report of the finances of the church, indicating that all responsibilities were cared for. But dad was astute enough to observe that the young pastor said nothing about his own salary. After the report was finished, the young preacher opened up the meeting for any questions or discussion, which was all the opening my father needed. He was not bothered by the fact that he was not a part of the local church as he stood and asked for a report on the pastor's salary. He remained standing as the young man stammered out a report that indicated several hundred dollars were lacking in payment of the church's responsibility to him. Dad kept talking as he walked toward the pulpit and then in a kind tone admonished the congregation on their obligations to the young pastor and his wife, telling them how unfair it was to send them away with unmet salary.

Dad pulled ten dollars out of his billfold, which was a generous gift in that day, and laid it on the communion table and suggested others do the same. People began coming from all over the congregation to put down money on the table. When it was all finished he picked it up and counted it out loud as the people watched him. He called the young pastor's wife forward to stand by her husband and then asked the chairperson of the church board to lead in a prayer of thanksgiving to God that the money had been raised. While they were praying, dad slipped out the door and no one ever knew who he was.

Now that's the kind of dad I had. Once when I would not allow a barber to cut my hair, he finally took me outside and wanted to know why I resisted the shears. I told him point blank, "I want to go back to that shop where they know my name." He not only laughed, but he took me back to the other barber shop, told the story hundreds of time, and always encouraged me to assert myself. I have loved selling from the days I was a child, and I learned it all from him. I guess I cannot separate what I am from the lovely mother and wonderful father God gave me.

And part of what I am belongs to my husband Les. We first met on a blind date at a meeting of our church in Oklahoma City. He spotted me a few weeks later in the registration line at Olivet College. Our first date was to play tennis that same afternoon and our lives have paralleled ever since. I suppose I owe much of my stability to him. He does not get upset as I do. He is much more philosophical about problems and people than I can ever hope to be. He is willing to let time do its work, and it does not seem to bother him much when he experiences turndowns and rejections. He just waits for another game on another field, and it seems always to come. After all these years of living together, I could never deny the fact that he is an important part of what I am.

Down underneath all the cultural conditioning, the relationships with the important people in my life, and the impact of good teachers and godly pastors, part of my life deep down under is unconditionally me. I am a special person God made and there is no one else like me in all the world. This unconditional me is not to be taken advantage of. It's my business to look after my own physical and spiritual welfare. We wives and mothers are usually the ones who care for the children and our husbands, but no one feels responsible to check on us. We make dental appointments for the rest of the family, arrange times for physical checkups, take the children to swimming lessons, encourage our husbands to jog, and plan nourishing meals. But who is going to look after me, unconditionally? Unless I do it, I am afraid it won't be done.

I am not complaining. I am one of the most favored people on earth. However, I think I have a God-given responsibility shared in common with every other woman in the world, to cultivate and motivate the unconditional me that is buried down beneath all of the accouterments that are a part of our complicated lives.

I have already told you that I am fulfilled in my role of hospitality in the home. That is my thing. I delight in keeping the home. I enjoy ease in entertaining, and for twenty-five years I have had pleasure in raising the children. The time and the place where I am most unconditionally me is in my own home when everyone else is gone and I have a quiet time that does not need to be shared with any other human being.

*First: I need to be unconditionally me in order to keep my senses.*

Lots of women have emotional problems. I am no psychologist and I do not even try to understand the dynamics of mental health that Les often talks about. I leave that up to him. But I know one thing, at least for me, that anything short of being unconditionally me drives me toward the emotional edge. I can only take care of everybody else's needs for so long before I have to take time for me. I can only meet everybody else's standards for so long and then something has to give. I fill a half-dozen roles or more as wife, mother, college president's spouse, seminar leader, chairperson of various committees and meetings, good neighbor, and household manager. But somewhere underneath all of these various roles that I happily accept and enjoy, there has got to be a time and place for me.

I want to be alive and secure. I don't like to live under the constant threat of physical breakdowns or the outrages of debilitating diseases. Recently, I stopped the merry-go-round and got off long enough to get a good physical rest, have a much needed checkup at the clinic, and get my dental work brought up to date. When I was all finished, I felt better about myself. It was not so much that the clinic found me healthy and the dentist found me hardy, as that I felt pleased with myself for taking enough time to look after me.

Then, I need to love and be loved. The evolution of love has brought me all the way from holding a helpless child in my loving arms to waving good-bye to my last son and his bride as I smiled on them with a healthy pride. I need the kind of love my husband can give me and the many ways I can love him. Romance is an attitude and not only a premarital event. I need to love people and have them love me. When I left the pastorate where I gave and received great amounts

**The time and place where I am most unconditionally me is in my own home.**

91

of love and became the wife of a college president who was expected only to pour tea and stay out of the way, the loss was severe enough to make its impact on my whole emotional system. My emotional being continued to be threatened until I found a way to compensate for the loss of one kind of love by replacing it with another. I guess this is what strength means to me: the capacity to adjust to the changing faces of love in our lives.

And, oh yes, I need to be simplistic in what I believe about God and his grace. I nearly dropped out of a master's degree program in religion once because I found it almost impossible to deal with the problems of higher criticism in the Bible. I know the two Isaiahs and the Johannine problem are important to the scholars, but I must just say frankly, they don't do anything for my faith. I just like to believe the Bible. I even enjoy reading the *Reader's Digest* version. I am not scandalized because they have left out some repetitious portions. The Bible is the greatest book in my life and I love it just as it is in all its versions. God, to me, is not a big white father-figure or some stern old gentleman on the outskirts of the endless universes. God is a spirit and as Jesus said, "Those who worship him must worship him in spirit and in truth." His grace is without limit and it applies to everything in my life. I love him because in Christ I do not need to have any more guilt. I am free to be me.

There are other needs in my life such as a craving for variety in my experiences. I like to travel. I like to meet new people. I like to see things I've heard about and I like doing things I've never done before. Also, I have a need for respect with a fairly good sense of self-worth and some occasional feelings of status. But the three most important needs in my life are the need to be alive and secure, the need to love and be loved, and the need to be simplistic in what I think about God and his grace.

*Second: To be unconditionally me, I must have a good sense of self-worth.*

Frankly, I have a struggle with all of the material I read and hear on loving myself. That sounds terribly egocentric and sub-Christian, even though the books are written by famous preachers as well as humanistic nonbelievers. But self-worth does make sense to me. To be unconditionally me, it is necessary that I have unconditional acceptance of myself as I am and that I feel this person who is me is a worthwhile individual.

I learned a long time ago that religious experience does not automatically guarantee emotional normalcy. Christians can also become neurotic and sometimes insane. Christians have nervous breakdowns, even those in the pulpit. I decided a long time ago that my chances for being a normal human being depended on the way the Holy Spirit could help me adjust to life as I have had it handed to me.

There is nothing academic about the free mental health examination I am about to offer you. But it has meant much to me through the years and has helped me as a reminder that I must continue to be unconditionally me.

• • •

• Are you genuinely happy? If you are miserable, that is one of the most important symbols signaling a poor mental adjustment.

• Do you have a zest for living? Or do you sit home and stare blankly at TV? Are you caught up in all of the soap operas and other kinds of escape mechanisms that keep you from facing reality? Or is the drama of your own life enough to keep you sparked and eager?

• Do you enjoy being with people? Loss of interest in people is a symptom of a vicious mental illness. God made us with a great gregarious spirit that can only be satiated by interacting with lots of wonderful people. When we start rejecting people we are actually rejecting another part of ourselves.

• Do you have unity and balance in your life?

• Can you live with each problem in your life as it arises or do you tend to go to pieces with each new difficulty?

• Do you have insight into your own conduct? Do you realize why you do what you do? Or do you simply blame all of your failures on other people who let you down? The beginning of all emotional wisdom is to say in its limitless applications to life, "I have a problem and I am responsible." People who accept responsibility for their problems are already on their way to workable solutions.

• Do you have a confidential relationship with at least one other person? A normal human being is one who has at least one relationship in life in which he or she can fully disclose himself or herself, let down and let go, and not be afraid of being hurt or victimized. Many people, however, go all the way through life without ever developing one relationship with another human being in which they have made themselves vulnerable. It is dangerous to have friends. It is even more dangerous to get married. It is dangerous to give yourself in loyalty to a church and its pastor. But not to do these things is worse.

• Can you genuinely laugh at things that happen to you?

• Are you engaged in satisfactory, fulfilling work? Or do you hate your work? If you hate housekeeping and find no fulfillment in staying at home, then the time has come for the unconditional me to make a decision and remedy an emotionally crippling problem. There are many kinds of opportunities for getting outside the home into work that is fulfilling. But if you do love your home and want to be there, don't allow anybody to intimidate you into leaving it for work in the marketplace unless you have overriding financial needs.

• Are you able to exert a measurable control over your

worries? Can you limit your worries to a given amount of time and then make a decision? Or do worries have a way of crippling your ability to decide?

• • •

*Third: To be unconditionally me I need self-knowledge.*

Since no one else in the world is just like me, I have the problem of getting to know and understand myself. What am I like as a human being and just what kind of a person am I? A person who does not have a realistic view of himself or herself is handicapped in meeting life's problems. I have known women who were as confused about themselves as an acorn would be if it were not sure whether its proper destiny was to be an oak or a cabbage. Some of these same women have unrealistic visions of life and distorted thoughts about themselves and their relationships to their husbands and to life because they do not know what it means basically to be human—what being human demands of them as well as gives to them.

Without adequate self-knowledge we may be confused as to who we are and feel a sense of being lost or that life is futile and we can only despair. Tragically, some women never come to terms with themselves and thus never recognize the way they really are. They remain unaware of annoying habits such as talking incessantly or continually belittling others. They drive away the very people they wish could be their friends and then feel hurt and bewildered by rejection. Some blame their failures on others while regarding themselves as faultless. They pay a heavy price for being unable to analyze and profit from their mistakes. They may be plagued by unnecessary worry about their innermost desires and thoughts. They may have fantasies that make them wonder if they are normal.

Some women try to solve this problem by assuming roles that are not genuine or authentic. Among Christians, the devil often gets people to assume false piety, attitudes of burden-bearing, or self-righteous humility that are neither genuine nor realistic. This drives away the unconverted, alienates such women from their family, and causes questions in the minds of fellow Christians who want to be supportive. Worst of all they become lost souls estranged from their own real self. Instead of being tranquil, confident, and secure, their inner thoughts are plagued by self-doubt, feelings of inadequacy, and anxiousness. The starting point in the growth and development of a Christian personality is to know what kind of person I am.

At those moments that I am most confident about the kind of person I am, I experiemce the twin results of confidence in the direction I am going and further confidence that the things I am doing are right for me. Goals focus my energy and efforts, guide the competencies I have developed, and provide the criteria for my decisions between alternate courses of action.

The problem of my personal goals is intimately related to values. It is important for me to know what kind of a life is good or bad for human beings in general and for me specifically. I keep asking myself the question, Am I willing to do what I am now doing for the rest of my life? Is what I am now doing helping fulfill God's purposes in my life?

For many women, living is a matter of muddling through. Literally millions of them guide their lives by superstitions or commonsense notions of human nature that science has proved to be false. They prepare for the wrong occupations, choose marriage partners on an irrational basis, and bring up their children with a naive hope that good intentions will be sufficient. But behind the brave front of confidence that they present to the world on Sunday morning are apt to be deep-seated feelings of bewilderment, inadequacy, and unhappiness. The price of muddling through is high. It takes a large toll in unnecessary failures, lost satisfactions, and emotional wear and tear on the human body, causing women to deteriorate ahead of their years. Violations of the laws of our nature are inevitably punished. No prosecutor is required. The wages of sin is death, if not to the person, certainly to our highest values and satisfactions. And ignorance of the law excuses none of us.

*Fourth: To be unconditionally me, I need the strength to cope.*

I once went to hear the famous heart specialist, Dr. Dudley White, speak to ten thousand women on the subject "Husbands and Heart Disease." He began by reporting on his immediate past experience at a hotel in San Francisco where he attended a seminar on the subject of stress and heart disease. He told about the long line of world-famous physicians and researchers who had been brought together to discuss the matter of stress and the heart. But like many academic convocations, the membership was thrown into immediate chaos five minutes after the opening discussion had begun when they could not agree among themselves on the meaning of stress. He said they argued all morning long and after the lunch break continued their search for the meaning of stress. He said that finally late in the afternoon, they came to a conclusion on a definition of stress that everyone was willing to live with, at least for the duration of the seminar, and it was this, "Stress is life and you had better like it."

**Stress is life and you had better like it.**

I do not know of any category of human beings who live under more stress than women. Our hormonal structure plus the conflicting demands made on our time often fly in the face of what we are and keep many of us under a kind of pressure, inner conflict, and frustration that adds up to continuing low-grade stress. This is why we contribute our fair share to the multibillion-dollar business of deodorants. Then we keep other international businesses profitable by buying cosmetics to cover up the lines that have come in our faces ahead of our years because of stress.

Pressures force us to intensify our efforts and to speed up our activities to an uncomfortable degree. These pressures we women feel may come from without or within—it really does not matter. The mind doesn't know the difference and the results are the same. Many women drive themselves mercilessly toward high levels of attainment that keep them under constant stress and strain. It is not the severe stress and strain of the moment that kills us, according to specialists in the field, but the low-grade stress that stays with us throughout the day and night. This kind of stress generates all sorts of sicknesses that tend to plague women over forty.

The effects of sustained distress on women vary considerably. What happens depends on whether the system is able to lessen the stress in some way or raise its tolerance. But with every woman, there is a point of no return. The breakdown does not come suddenly and without warning. It follows a very orderly progression.

• • •

• The woman on her way to a breakdown first goes through the alarm-reaction stage. This is a call-to-arms of the body's defense forces in face of physical and psychological stress. During this stage the chemical changes that mediate the body's ability to cope undergo changes as the nervous system mobilizes the human body to do battle.

• If the stressful situation continues, the alarm stage is typically followed by a stage of resistance in which the system apparently learns how to adapt to the particular stress. The symptoms that occurred during the alarm stage—such as headache, lower-back pain, or stomach discomfort—tend to disappear even though the stress continues. The hormones have smothered the symptom that originally signaled a problem and now the woman thinks she can continue staying up late at night, exerting inhuman effort, and somehow it will all work out because she is a good mother and a good wife.

• If the stress continues too long or becomes too severe, the bodily defenses of the woman will eventually break down, leading to a stage of exhaustion. The glands are no longer able to continue secreting their hormones at the increased rate, so that stress tolerance is lowered and whatever ability she had in fighting off the symptoms breaks down. Further exposure to this stress leads eventually to an emotional collapse or to a physically debilitating disease.

• • •

I live with a husband who probably handles more stress in stride without letting it get to him than anybody else I know. There may be many others like him, but he is the one I know best. He is not the victim of stress; he is a carrier. All our lives he has been a high-energy person. His jobs in the college president's office or in the pastor's study were demanding, or he made them that way. At one point in my early experiences when I was emotionally exhausted, a doctor told me I had two options: Either adjust to the stressful life-style that seemed to be ordered for my husband and me, or leave my family and go live alone in the country. Since the second option was totally unthinkable, I have learned to adjust myself and live with stress. I doubt if the stress in my life situation is any greater than yours. But I must tell you again, I could never carry on unless I had time to be unconditionally me, alone without interruption, resting, thinking, praying, and doing those things that give me the strength to cope.

# Meals from the Manse

BEING home for Christmas is one of the most important aspects of celebrating Christmas. One Christmas we brought all our children and parents to our home. There were scarcely any presents after paying for all the airline tickets, but everyone was home and that was the important thing about our celebration.

At our house, Christmas seems to be the only time of the year when we set up the projector and get out the slides. It is also the only time we stop long enough to make candy in our own kitchen. We seem to think about people at Christmas whom we have not contacted all year. So we send cards, make visits, send gifts, and make holiday calls. Christmas may be commercialized on Main Street, but in our home with our families there is always the warm spirit of friendship and goodwill. When members of the family are home, the Christmas music sounds sweeter, the decorations look prettier, the candles sparkle more brightly, and the fire is warmer and more cheerful.

But being home for Christmas is not always possible for everyone because of schedules, distances, and sometimes finances. I will always remember our first Christmas on the West Coast away from our families in the Midwest. The schedule and the money conspired to keep us from making the trip home.

The whole idea made us feel homesick, lonely, and beat. We overflowed with self-pity. We splurged on a better-than-usual hotel room and decorated it with a little tree. But it did not really help. We were away from home and we didn't like it. Nothing seemed to help. Finally, in the midst of all this loneliness and self-pity, Les made a pronouncement. He said we could either have an unhappy Christmas by keeping on like we were, or we could make a decision to make this a

**Chapter Fifteen**

Christmas to remember by doing something. We decided to make the decision in favor of a happy Christmas. In fact, Les had already decided that for us. All I had to do was go along with the idea. We adjusted our emotions and began casting about for a worthwhile project.

I told Les that I would like to write a book. He could have made fun of me, but he didn't. He just asked, "What kind of a book?" I thought a little while and then said I was interested in cooking and recipes and I would like to compile a cookbook. After more discussion, we finally realized that parsonage cooks are among the best in the world and those women should be the source for my recipes.

I was excited. The idea was taking on form. We began talking about a title that I knew had to be right. After dozens of suggestions we knew *Meals from the Manse* was right for what I wanted to do.

While I was at the library and bookstores the next day studying the layout of recipe books, Les composed a letter that explained the whole idea. I read the letter and it was good. He always could spell out an idea on paper better than I could.

Now we had a letter but we did not know where to send it. I had been hearing a lot about the Zondervan Publishing House in Grand Rapids, Michigan. So we decided they were the lucky people to whom we would send this idea. I got the address at the library and the letter was posted, just a few days before Christmas. Even if we never heard from them, we knew it was a good idea. And furthermore, it was a good Christmas. In using our creative energy to think of a worthwhile project, we had sloughed off despondency. Nearly every hour had been used in planning and working on the idea before and after the letter was mailed.

About the third morning after New Year's, we were awakened very early by a knock on the door of our motel. By now we were in Long Beach where Les was preaching in youth services. The manager was saying that Lora Lee Parrott had a telephone call in the office. I slipped into a robe and slippers and made my way to the office much concerned. Maybe something had happened in our family back East. Who would be phoning so early if it were not an emergency, and why would they be calling me and not Les? All these thoughts were racing through my mind.

When the operator said, "Grand Rapids, Michigan, calling," I still did not think of my letter to Zondervan. I must confess I was relieved and surprised when I learned the caller was Mr. Pat Zondervan. He said, "We like your *Meals from the Manse* and we want to publish it as soon as you can get it to us."

It was a Merry Christmas even if it was three days into the new year. For twenty-six years that cookbook sold consistently to many thousands of buyers. But I wonder if there would ever have been a *Meals from the Manse* if we had not decided to make ourselves happy and to turn our lonely holiday into a worthwhile project.

# I Met God in the Morning

I HAVE always liked sunrise better than sunset. There is something sad to me about the ending of a day, while the rising of the sun in the early morning hours is a harbinger of great things to come. There's more optimism in a sunrise than in a sunset. Maybe this is why I have always liked getting up early, preferably before Les and the boys, to have my own private time for meditation and prayer. It has been a habit throughout my adult years. I guess the place I love most has been our summer house on the coast of Maine. I love getting up to watch the first lobster boat break the water of the glassy bay. I am sure that is why I have always liked Bishop Cushman's poem about meeting God in the morning when the day is at its best. Since the first rays of the sun in the United States always fall on a mountain peak in Maine, I used to think about the remainder of the country still resting in darkness as I watched the sun come up over the ocean.

Thinking, praying, reading, and sometimes humming a hymn were my main bulwarks against whatever the day might hold. To me meditative reading of the Bible is different from study of the Bible. When I study the Bible I need to ask questions about the writer, the circumstances that motivated his words, place, time, and lots of other things the commentators say are important. Unfortunately for me, the more I study the Bible, the more I realize how limited the scope of my Bible knowledge is. But when it comes to meditative reading, I am a specialist. I can read as slowly or fast as I want to go at the moment, letting a single word or a whole paragraph say to me whatever God has to say at the moment. I am not trying to put anyone else under a guilt trip about getting up in the morning, but it just works that way with me. During the earliest hours of the day, I seem to identify most fully with the admonition, "Be still and know that I am God."

**Chapter Sixteen**

Praying in the early morning does several things for me:

• Getting up before everyone else for moments of quietness and prayer helps me to respond to the day instead of react to its demands. If I wait for the doorbell to chime or the phone to ring, I am then reacting instead of responding. To that degree somebody else is in charge of me. But with my private cup of coffee and my Bible, I can ease into the day, setting the pace that comes most naturally as I get the priorities in order.

• Getting up early helps me to give God first place in my life for that specific day. In the early morning, I can pray about things that may happen instead of those that already have. And I can give myself in a fresh new way to God instead of waiting for an SOS call after the pressures of the day have developed.

• When I pray early in the morning, I have a special clarity of thought and intention that seems to put things in proper order for everything else that is to come. I have never developed a checklist or written out priorities during this early-morning prayer time, but praying in the beginning moments of the day helps me put everything else in order.

• The early-morning hours seem to be the best time for me to praise God for his greatness and for me to meditate on his sacrifice and love to the world and especially to me. In the early-morning hours he does not restore peace; he gives peace.

• When I pray in the morning, God seems to give me some extra special blessings that I could not have any other time during the day. During the years the boys were small, one or more of them would often wake up very early. I enjoyed nothing more than a few moments to talk and pray and love the greatest gift God had given to me outside of his saving grace. Even before the baby got up, I had usually had my own private time. They just seemed to know when to wake up.

I am not suggesting that everyone needs to get up early in the morning in order to have a deep, abiding devotional relationship with God. Some women pray best at night. I know other women who always wait until their husband and children are out of the house at work and school before they have a quiet time alone.

*The Secret*

*I met God in the morning*
  *When my day was at its best,*
*And His presence came like sunrise,*
  *Like a glory in my breast.*
*All day long the Presence lingered,*
  *All day long He stayed with me,*
*And we sailed in perfect calmness*
  *O'er a very troubled sea.*
*Other ships were blown and battered,*
  *Other ships were sore distressed,*
*But the winds that seem to drive them*
  *Brought to us a peace and rest.*
*Then I thought of other mornings,*
  *With a keen remorse of mind,*
*When I too had loosed the moorings,*
  *With the Presence left behind.*
*So I think I know the secret,*
  *Learned from many a troubled way:*
*You must seek Him in the morning*
  *If you want Him through the day!*

*—Ralph Spaulding Cushman*

# Thoughts on Fashion

ONCE read that a New York designer said, "Take as many things off of a dress as you can." That suits me just fine because the clothes I like have simple lines and are plain cut. I dress to please my husband, and since he likes tailored things, his tastes have cut down sharply on my need for shopping time. I hardly look at frilly, dressy things. Classic lines and shirtwaist clothes stay in style from year to year, and it seems that a really good dress is worth wearing over and over again even from one season through the next. It does not take much imagination to add a smart new belt, a crisp bright scarf, or a beautiful lapel pin to change the look or give a tailored dress a little more dash. I always have felt that shoes are important. If I have one indulgence, it is in purchasing more shoes than I sometimes think I need. But just as important as buying shoes is the time, money, and effort needed to keep them in good repair. Smart-looking shoes with good soles and heels are almost always in fashion. There never has been much call for the run-down look. Although I enjoy wearing both low- and high-heeled sandals in the summertime, Les is most pleased when I wear a trim pair of high-heeled shoes with closed heels and toes, and almost no decoration. That is the classic pump—which he, of course, doesn't know—but it is easiest to obtain and I have ordered them many times on the telephone in the basic colors.

I think Les would send me right back to the beauty shop if I ever came home with a high-style, extreme hairdo. I once surreptitiously changed the color of my hair ever so slightly, month by month, until I was eventually blonde. But as soon as he caught on, it was back to the natural color. Still, keeping my hair trimmed and set has been a lifelong priority. It does not cost very much to keep your hair shampooed and in place.

**Chapter Seventeen**

**Attractiveness is ultimately an inside job.**

But there is more to a woman than clothes, shoes, and hair. Attractiveness is ultimately an inside job. Choosing the homecoming queen is an exciting event on our campus each October. During a recent queen's pageant, a beautiful girl was chosen. This was no surprise because the girls were beautiful every year. However, there was something inwardly special about this girl that caught the attention of many faculty and students. Everyone felt good about the choice. And yet, I could not help but notice that her wardrobe was much less expensive than former queens and less fashionable than the other girls in her court. This does not mean that her clothes were without taste, but noticeably of less quality. Her suits were not all wool and her dresses were synthetic blends, real compromises to anyone who is fashion conscious. However, this lack of sensitivity to fashion quality did not concern anyone, not even the queen herself. It was obvious that her real attractiveness was not in her feminine features or her straight teeth. She had about her a Christian winsomeness that could not easily be ignored. During the Sunday morning worship service she shared her Bible with me for the public reading of the Scripture and I noticed that her markings and study notes were on each page as we turned to follow the pastor's reading. It was not hard for me to understand the source of her real beauty. Her inner spirit was filled with love and kindness.

I have a friend who has said many times, "Fashion is not a price, but a look." I might add that fashion is not a price, but a sweet-spirited self-confidence in the Lord. I knew this was true after sharing the queen's Bible.

But now I want to tell you about another fashion that impressed me deeply. Actually, it was not a fashion at all, but a uniform, worn by a little thin woman who was surrounded by scores of children in the courtyard of her place in Bombay. Major Cook, as I came to know her, did not have the figure of a professional model. She was too short, too broad, and far too unsophisticated. But with Christian pride she wore the white dress uniform of the Salvation Army with its red and blue epaulets. Beneath her short-cropped naturally blonde hair was a well-scrubbed shining face accented by a pair of clear blue eyes. She was pure Scandanavian, thoroughly Christian, and everything about her was warmly straightforward. Like other fashionable clothes that are signed with the initials or signature of the designer, Major Cook had an "S" on each epaulet. The initials only accented the pure white spotless cotton from which the garment had been fashioned. It was belted and just the right length below the knee. The buttons down the front were pearl. The sleeves were short, and the collar was classic.

Her uniform might not have been considered high style in Paris or New York, but in a courtyard in Bombay, it was absolutely beautiful. There in quarters that were cramped beyond what is fair, Major Cook moved quietly among the

128 children in her custody. It was a startling experience to come past the picturesque squalor of the street people of Bombay into the walled yard filled with flowers and greenery. But getting to know Major Cook was even more impressive. She knew the names of each one of her children ranging in age from three months to fourteen years. At night, she kept the smallest ones in the room next to where she slept, always with the door open. She knew the cry of each child and could identify the nature of the cry, whether it was from physical hurt, loneliness, or just the human need for attention from her.

As we were taken through the compound, we were impressed with spotless cleanliness. Every bed was made without a wrinkle. We were taken to a kitchen where the older children prepared the curry meal for all of the others. As she said unobtrusively, "The children do everything." Checking on her good-naturedly. I pointed toward some three- and four-year-old children and said, "Who makes their beds?"

She said, "They do. They are taught from the time they can walk to make their beds each morning."

One very small boy named Ingmar, followed constantly. When we asked, she told us his story. He had been dropped off in her custody at age two because he had polio in both legs and had no further value to his family. Major Cook went to work massaging those little legs for one hour every six hours around the clock for many months—this besides all of her other work. She fashioned a cast for his legs to straighten them while he slept. Today he is running with those little legs and he sticks by her like a shadow. He is too little to understand, but somehow he must feel that his life and happiness are dependent on her.

It seemed as though my emotions were swinging in all directions. I pitied the children. But they were much better off than those on the streets. I wanted to take each child in my arms and say, God loves you and I only wish you knew how fortunate you are to have Major Cook.

Another child she pointed out was a little girl with only one arm. When she had broken her arm in an accident, the doctor had set the cast too tightly. Gangrene set in, and her arm had to be amputated at the shoulder. When the father saw that he could no longer marry off the girl for a price, he brought her to Major Cook and left her. She is a darling child. She had on a little red sweater with an empty sleeve. Her eyes were bright and she had pretty hair, and was sharp in every way.

Many more stories could be told about Major Cook's work. One interesting thing about this heroic lady is that she never changes her wardrobe, year in and year out. She wears that same white dress, the one with the epaulets, the dress with the fashion designer initials "S S" which stand for "saved to serve"

I do not believe we are going to wear "S S" on our dresses or suits. But I think we could take a page out of the book of the Salvation Army and say, "My clothes must quietly say, "S S." I'm saved to serve and I want to look my fashionable best. I want to be a conservative Christian, but I also want to look nice enough to send the message of my heart that I am saved to serve.

# A Speaker I Am Not

## Chapter Eighteen

SOMEWHERE in my files is a speech on the subject "Children in the Parsonage." The manuscript is full of information and lists of successful preachers' children who became senators, lawyers, university presidents, writers, doctors, and entertainers. It contains many profound quotes concerning life in the parsonage.

A lot of work went into that speech because it was the first speech I ever made. I was invited several hundred miles away from home to speak before a banquet of pastors and their wives. I was scheduled for the closing session of their conference.

The banquet hall looked enormous. I was overwhelmed and could not eat. I could not make dinner conversation at the head table where they seated me because I was too anxious about how I would come across as a speaker. Sometimes the sound of the table conversation mixed with laughter made me feel like the whole situation was unreal and maybe I was just dreaming.

However, I got through the evening, reading my speech with a fair amount of freedom. As I reviewed it later, I realized I had not really helped anyone by what I said. No one had received any new thoughts. Certainly no one was going to make any decisions or act in any new way that would improve their lives. All I had done was entertain and impress them, or so I hoped.

Then I began to listen to speakers more carefully. I came to the conclusion that anyone who gave a speech on something they really believed in made much more impact on the audience than those who just spoke because they knew how. After hearing all the speakers at a church conference, I came to the conclusion that those who had a nice message but did not feel it deep inside, had made hollow sounds and had left the people unmoved. But those who spoke from conviction came across much more effectively. I even observed that the chairpersons who made the announcements and admonitions with real conviction were much more credible than those who did not.

As I began to realize the great need to speak on subjects I really believed in, the fear of speaking began to leave me. From then on I limited my talking to subjects I really knew about and cared about sincerely, such as parsonage life, hospitality, children, homemaking, and personal devotional living. I could talk about a lot of things but these were the subjects I could deal with from experience and conviction.

I am not, academic. Although I have a master's degree, I long since learned that trying to quote the authorities and match one set of research against another was not for me. I have not lived these years in an ivory tower, but in a house full of action and four demanding males, one grown and the other three trying to be. So, whatever I talk about must come from my own experience.

Another thing I had to learn about speaking was voice modulation. I had an idea that a strong, well-modulated voice was one of the keys to successful speaking. A woman I know takes on a stained-glass voice and sounds like a prophet when she speaks. I love to hear her. But a conversational tone, projected to the person in the last row, so all may hear, is most comfortable for me. It is hard for me to take on any false accents and stage pronunciations when I am talking about our Siamese cat. I just might as well be me when I tell how she was found in our garage crying like a baby, how the whole family heard it, fed the cat, and adopted her as our own. No false voices are needed to tell that kind of story—it just wouldn't fit.

So eventually, my place in speaking began to be clear to me. If I can help people, I am glad to speak. Otherwise it is not worth my time and especially the time of the audience.

A woman has a lot more to think about than just her speech. I have to be sure that my hair is fixed and that I have an appropriate dress for the occasion. I need to leave things in order for the family at home. I am not crazy about trying to get on the right flight in a huge airport by myself. And if the motel or hotel is not first class I don't sleep well. Bad places to stay leave me with all kinds of imaginary fears.

I've seen Les leave for a whole weekend of speaking with only one little case, straight from the office. He has no hair problems, no clothes decisions, and no worry about the food stocked in the refrigerator back home. He knows the airline gates and has no fear of riding in a cab alone in a strange city at night. He likes a good hotel as well as I do but adjusting to mediocrity does not seem to interfere with his sleep. As far I as can tell he sleeps just as well in a second-rate place as he does in a world-class hotel.

So this is why I never aspire to a speaking schedule. Others may like to go on the road telling their story, and I think they should, by all means. I love to hear the good speakers who come and go across our campus each year. But as for me, a speaker I am not. I much prefer to exercise my gift of hospitality in the home and on the campus of the college I love.

# New Horizons
# and
# Fresh Resources

*And the glory of the Lord came into the house by the way of the gate whose prospect is toward the east.*

*—Ezekiel 43:4*

# A Personal Word About Horizons and Resources

SINGERS have their repertoire. Speakers have their outlines. Teachers have their syllabi. Mechanics have their tools. But home executives who find fulfillment in hospitality have their resources. These resources have usually been honed and refined across the years by the limit of our social horizons and serving resources. I do not try to fill the gamut of all possible kinds of entertaining. I do not need to. But through the years of attending and generating hospitality events I have come to count on some things from hostesses who predictably do well in whatever social event they attach themselves. These are people who have helped me to lift my horizons and develop some willing resources.

The best cooks and the most gracious hostesses I have observed are Christian laywomen and pastor's wives. Without the help of servants, caterers, and homes with rooms like banquet halls, they produce results that are dependent on their cooking skills, the gracious way they organize their serving, and the imaginative ways they prepare a table. Their food is always wholesome and ranges from tasty to elegant. Their ways are winsome and their manners are not on parade but always demonstrate sensitivity to their guests. They know how to use flowers, colors, and arrangements without depending on sterling and crystal. Some of the hostesses have both, but the success of their hospitality is not dependent on expensive tableware. I admire these people and always love to be invited to their homes where hospitality is a hallmark.

My resources are mostly what I have learned from these gracious hostesses, mostly in homes but sometimes in restaurants. I hope the menu suggestions and the recipes that follow will do for you what they have done for me. They will be winners if prepared properly and served in the ambience that is represented by all that warm Christian hospitality stands for.

# A Reception with a Regal Touch

YEARS ago Les and I were invited for an interview with a congregation in California. The session with the board was followed by a tour of their beautiful church. When we went into the sanctuary Les invited the board members and spouses to be seated while he talked with them from the pulpit. As I remember, he spoke with them briefly about the role of the pastor and the layperson. Then he quoted some Scripture to try out the acoustics, reduced his last Sunday morning sermon to no more than five minutes, and closed with prayer.

At the end of this devotional moment a young woman whose attractive ways have always stuck in my mind, stood and turned the attention of all of us to a reception she and her committee had prepared for the prospective pastor and his wife and the church board couples. Church receptions held in annexes and lower levels often leave much to be desired for obvious reasons. They are usually multi-purpose rooms with inadequate storage space or the lack of will to get the room dividers, bulletin board contents, and other distractions out of sight. If the room doubles for a gym or recreational area, the echo is often a problem and candles on a table under the backboard at one end of the basketball court can seem like an anachronism. Usually, the room is too large or too small. But Jean had taken care of all these usual problems in the way she made the table the central focus. Her use of lighting included both candles and lamps to create a very cozy atmosphere for about forty people. Jean did not regiment the people into a line that went past the table cafeteria style but suggested everyone visit with one another and go to the table as they desired. The Lord did not seem to lead Les and me to accept their invitation to be their pastor, but Jean and the rest of those people made a long term impression on me with the gracious way they turned a routine church board reception into a memorable expression of Christian hospitality.

One fresh idea Jean had was a unique collection of absolutely delectable cookie bars. In fact, the only sweet things on the table were these bars of pure goodness offered on similar large round plates at one end of the table near the tea and coffee service. Someone who does not get fulfillment from hospitality may feel it was too much bother to coordinate the bringing of cookie bars by woman of the church. But I'm glad Jean did not think it was too much bother to do well what she had been asked to do in a church reception. It would have been easier and probably cheaper to buy a variety of bags of assorted cookies at the supermarket. But in these following six recipes, Jean and the women of the board in this California church set themselves apart as hostesses with new horizons and fresh resources. With a half-dozen options, I'm sure everyone had their favorite. Mine was the dream bars. They were so light and tasty they nearly floated. Les, as I knew without watching his plate, did best by the lemon bars. But, then, he likes everything with a lemon taste, even wedges of fresh lemon without anything else.

> **The only sweet things on the table were a unique collection of absolutely delectable cookie bars.**

## Dream Bars

*¼ cup shortening*
*½ cup brown sugar*
*1 cup flour*

Mix together and pat in bottom of square pan.
Bake 10 minutes at 325°.
Then prepare the following:

| | |
|---|---|
| *2 tbsp. flour* | *½ tsp. baking powder* |
| *¼ tsp. salt* | *1 cup chopped walnuts* |
| *1 cup flaked coconut* | *2 eggs* |
| *1 tsp. vanilla* | *1 cup brown sugar* |

Sift flour, salt, and baking powder over nuts and coconut. Mix 2 eggs and 1 cup brown sugar and vanilla and add to first mixture. Spread evenly over baked crust. Bake 15 to 20 minutes at 325°.

## Nutty Nuggets

*¾ cup shortening, rounded*
*1¾ cup sifted flour*
*4 tbsp. sugar*
*¼ tsp. salt*
*1 tsp. vanilla*
*1½ cup nuts, chopped*

Cream sugar and shortening. Sift flour and salt into shortening mixture. Add vanilla and nuts; roll into logs and bake at 350° for 15 minutes. Cool 3 minutes. Roll in powdered sugar.

## Best-Ever Brownies

Oil and flour a 9 x 13 x 2-inch baking dish and preheat oven to 350°.
Beat together:
> *4 eggs and 2 cups sugar*

Melt in saucepan:
> *1 cup shortening and 6 rounded tbsp. cocoa*

Combine above ingredients and add:
> *1½ scant cup flour*
> *dash of salt (less than ⅛ tsp.)*
> *1 cup chopped nuts*
> *1 tsp. vanilla*

Bake for 30 minutes at 350°. Frost with Fudge Frosting when cool, if you care to.

## Fudge Frosting

> *1 package confectioners sugar (1 lb.)*
> *½ cup cocoa*
> *¼ tsp. salt*
> *⅓ cup boiling water*
> *⅓ cup butter, softened*
> *1 tsp. vanilla*

Combine sugar, cocoa, and salt. Add boiling water and butter. Blend. Stir in vanilla. Frost cookie bars.

## Crispy Candy Bars

> *1 cup Karo light or dark corn syrup*
> *1 cup sugar*
> *1 cup Skippy chunky-style peanut butter*
> *6 cups crisp rice cereal (Rice Krispies)*
> *1 small pkg. chocolate pieces, 6 oz.*
> *1 small pkg. butterscotch pieces, 6 oz.*

**Jean did not think it was too much bother to do well what she had been asked to do in a church reception.**

Mix Karo and sugar in sauce pan. Bring to boil over medium heat, stirring frequently. Remove from heat. Stir in peanut butter and cereal. Press mixture into a well-greased pan 13 x 9 x 2 inches. Melt chocolate and butterscotch pieces. Spread over top of cereal mixture. Cool. Cut into 1″ x 2″ bars. Makes about 54 pieces.

## Magic Cookie Bars

*½ cup butter or margarine, melted*
*1½ cup graham cracker crumbs*
*1 cup walnuts coarsely chopped*
*1 cup semisweet chocolate chips (6 oz. pkg.)*
*1⅓ cup flaked coconut (3½ oz. can)*
*1 can Eagle Brand condensed milk (14 oz.)*

Pour melted butter onto the bottom of a 13 x 9 x 2-inch pan. Sprinkle crumbs evenly over melted butter. Sprinkle chopped nuts evenly over crumbs. Scatter chocolate pieces over nuts. Sprinkle coconut evenly over chocolate pieces. Pour sweetened condensed milk evenly over coconut. Bake in a 350° oven for 25 minutes or until lightly browned on top. Cool in pan 15 minutes. Cut into bars.

## Lemon Bar Cookies

*1 cup flour*
*½ cup butter or margarine*
*¼ cup powdered sugar*
*¼ tsp. salt*

Cream butter, sugar, flour and salt. Pat into a greased baking dish (10 inches square) and bake 15 to 20 minutes at 350°
Combine and pour over hot crust at once:

*2 eggs, slightly beaten*
*1 cup sugar*
*¼ tsp. baking powder*
*2 tbsp. flour*
*2 tbsp. lemon juice and grated rind of half a lemon*

Bake at 350° for 20 to 25 minutes. Remove from oven and sprinkle on top ¾ cup powdered sugar that has been mixed with the juice of lemon half.

# Mom's Cherry Pie and Lemon Cake

LES and I were married when he was old enough to vote and I was not. By today's standards that may seem a bit young but with us it has worked out great. One of the reasons may be that we very soon left our parents behind and began making a wonderful life for ourselves in the Northwest. But for more than twenty-five years, until Les came back to Olivet as president of the college, we made intermittent trips to see his mom and dad, who lived close to the campus.

These visits to see Dr. and Mrs. Parrott, Sr., were never more than two nights long and mostly an overnight event. But it never mattered how long we stayed, or whether we came in cold or warm weather, the central celebration of our reunion was always around a bountiful dinner table. Les has a brother, John, who is a surgeon in Minneapolis and a sister, the wife of the late Dr. Ralph Perry, who lived across the street from her parents. On occasion his brother or sister or both would be on hand for these Parrott reunions, but one thing never changed regardless of who was there or the time of year in which the event was held. Even if we came three or four times a year, we always wanted the same menu: baked swiss steak, pan-fried chicken simmered in the skillet, cornbread sticks, and all of the fresh vegetables that were in season. If we were there for two nights, we usually had swiss steak one evening and chicken the other. If we were only going to be there for one night, we asked for both of them at the same meal.

When it came to dessert time, we had a saying around the Parrott table, that the sweetest words in the English language are: "Keep your fork." No one could ever make cherry pie or lemon gelatin cake like Les's mother.

One of our best family stories concerns one of these cherry pies that Les's mother fixed for him to take home on the

**We always wanted
the same menu:
baked swiss steak,
pan-fried chicken
simmered in the
skillet, cornbread
sticks, and all the
fresh vegetables in
season.**

plane to the Pacific Northwest. It was unbaked and ready for me to stick into the oven on his arrival. It seemed like a good idea at the time. Howard Hamlin and Mark Moore, for some reason I cannot remember, were driving him to the O'Hare airport which at the time was torn up with one of Mayor Daley's big reconstruction programs. Realizing their time was almost gone, Howard took charge and told Mark and Les to make a run for it and he would stay with the car. The terminal was nearly a half mile away. Mark carried the suitcase and Les carried the unbaked cherry pie through and around all of the mud puddles that had developed from the spring rains. Les made the plane all right but he would not have without Mark making arrangements with the agent at the counter to call the gate and ask them to hold the door for one more passenger. The friendly skies were cooperative and Les ran up the steps with his suitcase and pie. The passengers cheered as he turned to go down the aisle into the coach section. I met him at the airport that evening and before we went to bed, we enjoyed a cherry pie worth carrying across the United States for hand delivery.

As for the lemon gelatin cake, I have already told you how Les likes anything with the flavor of lemon. It must be a family tradition from Tennessee. At least no one in his house ever grew tired of his mother's lemon gelatin cake. I doubt that you will, either.

## Lemon Gelatin Cake

*1 package of lemon gelatin (3 oz.)*
*1 cup of boiling water (dissolve gelatin and let cool)*
*4 eggs*
*¾ cup of vegetable oil*
*Dash of salt*
*1 package of lemon or yellow cake mix*

Beat eggs lightly, add oil, salt, gelatin mixture, and cake mix. Beat two minutes on medium speed. Pour into 9 x 13 x 2½-inch pan. Bake at 350° for 30 to 45 minutes. When baked, pierce cake all over every two inches. Mix two cups confectioners sugar with ½ cup reconstituted lemon juice, and pour over cake while still hot. This creates a glaze after the cake has cooled so that no icing is needed. Should be prepared a day or two before desired serving time to let flavor improve.

# Cherry Pie

*1 cup sugar*
*1½ tbsp. quick cooking tapioca*
*¼ tsp. salt*
*1 can pitted tart red cherries, unsweetened*
*1 tbsp. butter*
*Pastry for double crust*

Combine sugar, tapioca, and salt; stir in the cherry juice. Add the cherries and let stand while making pastry dough.

Line 9-inch pie plate with pastry; fill with cherry mixture. Dot with butter. Place top crust and crimp edges. Bake in hot oven (450°) for ten minutes. Reduce to 350° and bake 30 to 45 minutes more.

# Chicken Salad Supreme

*O*NE of the sweetest people I know is Fran Pannier, who has lived most of her adult life in Wisconsin church parsonages. She has never had a lot to work with but she has not needed it in order to demonstrate her infectious spirit of hospitality. Typical of her fresh resources is this chicken salad supreme. It is not only good to the palate, but it just sounds good on paper.

## Chapter Twenty-Two

## Chicken Salad Supreme

*3 cups cooked chicken*
*1 cup green grapes, halved*
*¹/₂ cup toasted almonds*
*¹/₂ cup chopped celery*
*3 tbsp. chopped onion*
*¹/₂ tsp. celery salt*

Fold ingredients into dressing (below). Serve on lettuce. Garnish with frosted green grapes.

*Dressing:*
*¹/₃ cup mayonnaise*
*¹/₃ cup lemon yogurt*
*¹/₂ tsp. prepared mustard*

*Garnish:*
*Brush some green grapes with beaten egg white.*
*Dip into dry lime gelatin.*
*Dry on rack.*

# An Authentic Mexican Dip

REALLY good authentic dip to use with corn chips is Chile con Queso. That is pronounced chilly-con-kay-so. The ingredients are as follows:

## Chapter Twenty-Three

### Chile con Queso

*1 lb. Velveeta, cut into small cubes*
*1 can (4 oz.) green chiles, diced*
*1 can (1 lb.) whole tomatoes, drained, then chopped fine*
*1 tbsp. dried minced onions*

Heat all ingredients together in chafing dish over boiling water until cheese is melted and it is hot. Serve with corn chips.

**A good authentic dip to use with corn chips is Chile con Queso.**

# Where's the Barbecue?

F you came over to my house for leftovers on Monday after one of our Sunday roast beef dinners, you would likely get some of the best barbecue sandwiches you ever tasted in your life. The recipe is not mine, but it goes back so far I really don't know where it came from, probably Texas where our family has lots of relatives. If I tried a substitute for the roast on Sunday I could count on my family having their own version of "Where's the beef?" And anything but sandwiches from the leftovers on Monday would evoke, "Where's the barbecue?" I hope you like this sauce as much as we do.

## Chapter Twenty-Four

## Barbecue Sauce

*1 tbsp. butter*
*1 medium onion, minced*
*1 small clove garlic, minced*
*1 bottle of catsup (12-14 oz.)*
*½ cup vinegar*
*2 tbsp. brown sugar*
*¼ tsp. cayenne pepper*
*1 tsp. Worcestershire sauce*
*¼ tsp. allspice*

In a saucepan, melt butter and add minced onion and garlic. Cook over medium heat until golden brown, three to five minutes.

Add the catsup, vinegar, brown sugar, and cayenne pepper.

Cook all ingredients over medium heat for half an hour. Stir frequently or until sauce is reduced by a third.

**If you come over to my house for leftovers on Monday, you would likely get some of the best barbecue sandwiches you ever tasted in your life.**

# Lawry's Prime Rib Restaurant

FIRST got acquainted with Lawry's marvelous Prime Rib Restaurant years ago when they asked me to do an endorsement for their seasoning salt after the publication of my cookbook, *Meals from the Manse*. When Les and I visited their restaurant, I saw immediately that they had both new horizons and fresh resources.

Lawry's was the first restaurant in America to serve a tossed green salad before the main course, starting a major trend in American dining habits. And they helped make the baked potato famous as a specialty. They introduced the single entree menu in their Lawry's Prime Rib Restaurant in Beverly Hills and repeated it in the old mansion they converted into a Lawry's Prime Rib at Ontario and Michigan Avenue in Chicago.

For nearly fifty years, they have been doing one thing extremely well, good enough to keep people backed up waiting for seats. They never tell the complete secret on how they produce high-quality prime rib day after day. For one thing, however, it is cooked in rock salt which must be broken off with a metal tool after it has been cooked. Also, they cook the meat very slowly and obviously have the best quality cuts.

However, Lawry's is willing to share their recipe for creamed spinach which I have served many, many times. I have noticed through the years that most people take seconds. Also, their Yorkshire pudding can't be beat. I have never eaten any other Yorkshire pudding that equals it.

## Chapter Twenty-Five

## Creamed Spinach A La Lawry's

*1 package frozen chopped spinach, (10 oz.)*
*2 slices bacon, finely chopped*
*½ cup finely chopped onion*
*2 tbsp. flour*
*1 tsp. Lawry's seasoned salt*
*¼ tsp. Lawry's seasoned pepper*
*1 clove garlic, minced\**
*1 cup milk*

Cook spinach according to package directions. Drain well. Fry bacon and onions together until onions are tender, about 10 minutes. Remove from heat. Add flour, seasoned salt, seasoned pepper, and garlic. Blend thoroughly. Slowly add milk, return to heat, and stir until thickened. Add spinach and mix thoroughly. Makes 4 servings.

*\*or ¼ tsp. Lawry's Garlic Powder with Parsley.*

## Yorkshire Pudding

*1 cup, less 1 tsp., sifted flour*
*½ tsp. salt*
*2 eggs, beaten*
*¾ cup milk*
*¼ cup water*

Sift flour and salt together; make a well, add eggs. Blend together, then add milk and water slowly, beating continuously. If using an electric mixer, beat at high speed for at least 10 minutes.\* Let stand for an hour. Heat oven to 450°. Place a 5-inch omelette pan in oven to heat. When hot, coat the pan with oil, heat again. Pour ½ cup batter into pan; bake for 35 minutes. Makes 4 servings.

*\* Very important to beat a long time.*

## Salad Bowl A La Lawry's

*1 small head romaine*
*1 small head iceberg lettuce*
*½ cup watercress, torn in sprigs*
*1 cup shoestring beets, well drained*
*1 hard-cooked egg, sieved*
*Lawry's seasoned salt*
*Lawry's seasoned pepper*
*¾ cup Lawry's Famous French Dressing*
*6 cherry tomatoes*

Tear romaine and lettuce into pieces. Add watercress, beets, and eggs. Sprinkle with seasoned salt and seasoned pepper. Toss with Famous French Dressing. Place 1 cherry tomato on each plate with serving of salad. Makes 6 servings.

# Strawberry Cookies

JUSTINE and John Knight are really from Tennessee, although they have lived in lots of places where John has served as preacher, teacher, editor, and college president. But I have a feeling Justine's southern ways come through in some marvelous strawberry cookies she makes that are almost like a candy confection. They are not only good but they make an interesting tray on the tea table or as a side accompaniment to a serving of quality ice cream.

### Strawberry Cookies

*1 can Eagle Brand sweetened condensed milk (14 oz.)*
*3 packages strawberry gelatin (3 oz.)*
*2 packages flaked coconut (approximately 7 oz. each)*
Method:

Mix condensed milk, 2-½ packages gelatin, and 2 packages coconut. Refrigerate 8 hours. Form into strawberry shapes. Roll the strawberries in the remaining gelatin. Break a toothpick in half and color with green food color for stems. Cut green gum drops in thin and flat leaf shapes and roll in sugar. Attach leaves to berry with the toothpick stem.

# *Gwen's Broccoli Casserole*

## Chapter Twenty-Seven

IT was a good day for me when Les and I were invited to the home of Janice and David Brunkal, who at that time lived in Portland, Oregon. It was the Christmas season and they had just moved into their first house. Janice had invited her two brothers and their wives and her mom and dad. So there was really a big table of us ready to make the most of the season of the year and the hospitality of Janice and David.

Since it was a family affair, Gwen had brought a casserole brimming full with broccoli and cheese. I will always be glad she did. I suppose I have served this one vegetable dish to more guests in our home and in the president's dining room than any other vegetable dish. It is like eating olives. One serving calls for another. However, let me give you a warning: the secret is in the Velveeta cheese and Ritz crackers. No substitute ingredients will work together like they do in this recipe. Believe me, I have tried it.

### Broccoli Casserole

*2 boxes frozen chopped broccoli (10 oz. each)*
*1 stick butter (¼ lb.)*
*½ lb. Velveeta cheese*
*¼ lb. Ritz crackers*

Cook broccoli as directed on package; drain. Add ½ stick butter, ½ lb. Velveeta cheese. Stir until cheese dissolves. Put in greased casserole. Crush ¼ lb. Ritz crackers, mix with ½ stick melted butter. Spread over top. Bake at 350° 20-30 minutes.

# Dick Willis's Sweet and Sour

DICK Willis is one of the nicest men I have ever known. He must have broken the hearts of lots of women because he has remained single all these many years, first as a bank executive, and now, as a dollar-a-year man helping his local church and district organization to run more effectively.

Dick lives in a very large California ranch-style house complete with a big swimming pool and lots of recreation area. All of his friends know that he keeps this big layout just so that he can entertain in the typical Dick Willis fashion. He has class and he knows how to get things done, ordinarily without a caterer or any hired help. Dick is everybody's favorite and all the people I know always look forward to an invitation to his house. The sweet and sour pork explained below is a typical Dick Willis dish for a large crowd, followed by his favorite dessert, Philadelphia cream cheese pie.

**Chapter Twenty-Eight**

### Sweet and Sour Chicken*

8 tbsp. cornstarch
8 tbsp. flour
3 cups brown sugar
4 medium green pepper (chopped)
4 cans of pineapple chunks (15 oz.)
2 cups of vinegar
1 large bottle catsup
2 onions diced or dried
28 whole chicken breasts, boned

*pork can also be used

Boil chicken breasts and cool. Mix flour and cornstarch with some of cooking liquid before adding other ingredients. Add cut-up chicken. Cook at low heat for 45 minutes or longer. (The longer it cooks, the better it tastes.)

Very easy to make—the large portions can be made in a roasting pan. Additional amounts of the ingredients can be added to suit the taste. Serve over white rice. Serves 50.

## Philadelphia Cream Cheese Pie

Crust:
> *½ cup sugar*
> *1 cup pretzel crumbs*
> *¼ cup butter*

Filling:
> *2 packages Dream Whip topping mix*
> *8 oz. package Philadelphia Cream Cheese*
> *⅓ cup powdered sugar*
> *1 cup cold milk*

Crust: Mix together and press in 9-inch pie pan; put in freezer.

Filling: Whip ingredients with electric mixer according to whipped topping directions. Spread on chilled pretzel mix, then freeze again. When ready to serve, cover with 1 can cherry or blueberry pie filling (about 21 oz.).

May be kept in refrigerator several days. Serve frozen or partially melted. If a 9 x 13-inch dish is used, double the recipe.

# Jill Bowling's Cheesecake

*L*OTS of people buy cheesecake in restaurants, but only a few people have enough skill and nerve to make it at home. Our pastor's wife, Jill Bowling, is this kind of cook. You might consider yourself fortunate ever to be invited to her home across the street from the Burke Administration building on the campus of Olivet. She and her husband took on the enormous job of restoring the gracious old Frank Lloyd Wright style house that has been occupied through the years first, in 1903, by a French-Canadian family with nine children, then by the priests of the Viatorian order, and finally by the music department of Olivet Nazarene College. What they have achieved is difficult to describe in ordinary words. And if you do ever get invited to their house, just hope that she may serve you a piece of her delicious cheesecake.

## Chapter Twenty-Nine

### Jill Bowling's Cheesecake

Crust:
> 2 cups crushed graham crackers
> 1 tbsp. sugar
> 1 stick butter, softened (¼ lb.)

Mix well and press into the bottom of a 10-inch springform pan.

Filling:
> 3 packages cream cheese, softened (8 oz. each)
> 5 eggs
> 1 cup sugar
> 1¼ tsp. vanilla

Mix together, adding one egg at a time, until smooth. Pour filling into pan and bake for 1 hour at 300°. Take from oven. Let stand while making topping.

Topping:

*1 pint sour cream*
*½ cup sugar*
*1¼ tsp. vanilla*

Mix and pour over top; return cheesecake to oven at 300° for 5 minutes. Refrigerate overnight. Garnish with strawberries or sliced kiwi fruit.

# A Michigan Treat

_O_UR daughter-in-law served us a delicious rhubarb pie. She said that their congregation was blessed with many good cooks, both men and women. This one comes from Yvonne Spencer, a super hostess.

### Rhubarb Pie

_2 ½ cups rhubarb_
_1¼ cups sugar_
_3 tbsp. flour_
_3 eggs_
_½ tsp. cinnamon_
_1 cup milk_
_3 tbsp. melted butter_

Mix sugar and flour with the rhubarb. Spread rhubarb mixture on the bottom of the pie crust (see below). Beat eggs, cinnamon, milk, and butter together and pour over rhubarb. Bake at 400° for 5 minutes then 350° for 25 to 30 minutes.

### Pie Crust

_1 stick butter (¼ lb.)_
_1 cup flour_
_1 tbsp. sugar_

Mix and pat in pie plate. Bake at 350° for 10 minutes.

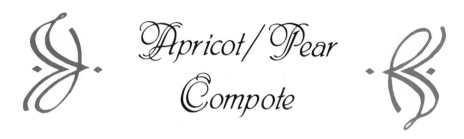

# Apricot/Pear Compote

DONNA Spittal, whose husband is a superintendent of schools in Fort Wayne, Indiana, has had a lot of experience in Christian hospitality both in their home, at official functions, and in her church. As a different dessert, her apricot-pear compote is especially appreciated by those who spurn pastry.

## Chapter Thirty-One

### Apricot-Pear Compote

*1 can pears, drained and sliced (29 oz.)*
*½ cup dried apricots, halved*
*¼ cup sugar*
*¼ cup plus 2 tbsp. orange juice*
*¼ cup sliced maraschino cherries*
*⅛ tsp. ground nutmeg*

In a 1½-quart casserole, combine all ingredients. Cover and chill in the refrigerator at least 1 hour (overnight is better). Bake covered at 325° for 50 to 60 minutes or until apricots are tender. Serve warm.

# Japanese Stack-Ups

I T was our youngest son's own idea to attend a preparatory school in Kansas City named Barstow. The one problem was where to stay, since the private high school had no boarding facilities. The answer came from our good friends, Jim and Bev Smith, who lived in nearby Olathe, Kansas. Jim had been our coach at the college in New England. They had a son, Greg, the same age as our Les III, and the friendship between our two families had grown through the years. It was as natural for Beverly to offer their home for Les III while he attended school as it was for us to accept. And for him, one of the highlights during his years in their home was Bev's excellent cooking. Even after he was in college at Mid-America, he still dropped by for Sunday dinner unannounced. He said he could just picture what it was going to be like all during the Sunday morning service and by the time the benediction was prayed he had talked himself into being an uninvited guest. They must not have objected because this became a weekly event.

From Bev Smith I got one of the best recipes I have ever had to turn an ordinary women's luncheon into a special event. I have served her Japanese stack-ups with curried harvest fruit for dessert to women's luncheons of no more than ten as well as to four hundred people. Since this is a do-it-yourself kind of lunch that invites people to return to the serving table, there is ample opportunity for seconds and sometimes thirds. I am indebted to Beverly for both the menu and the recipes.

**Chapter
Thirty-Two**

## Japanese Stack-Ups

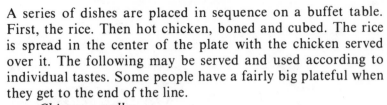

A series of dishes are placed in sequence on a buffet table. First, the rice. Then hot chicken, boned and cubed. The rice is spread in the center of the plate with the chicken served over it. The following may be served and used according to individual tastes. Some people have a fairly big plateful when they get to the end of the line.

> *Chinese noodles*
> *hot crushed pineapple*
> *green pepper, diced*
> *green onion, chopped*
> *diced celery*
> *Mandarin oranges*
> *grated hard-cooked eggs*
> *coconut, shredded*
> *raisins*
> *slivered almonds*

At the end of the line, position a chicken supreme sauce to pour over the whole dish. More hot sauce may be served in gravy boats at the tables.

## Chicken Supreme Sauce

> *Canned condensed cream of mushroom soup or cream of celery*
> *Evaporated milk or cream (to thin)*

Heat soup, thin with cream. (Don't let it get too thin.) Serve over stack-ups.

Another recipe from Beverly Smith is this one:

## Curried Harvest Fruit

> *1 package mixed dried fruit (12 oz.)*
> *1 can pineapple chunks, undrained (13¼ oz.)*
> *1 can cherry pie filling (21 oz.)*
> *¼ cup water*
> *½ to 1 tsp. curry powder*

Cut large pieces of dried fruit in half. Combine pie filling, water, and curry powder. Pour over fruit. Cover and bake at 350° for 1 hour. Serves 10.

# An Alternative to Red Meat

ACCORDING to the National Heart, Lung, and Blood Institute, heart attacks caused an estimated sixty billion dollars in medical bills, lost wages, and lost productivity last year, which is more than the total Medicare budget. This fact, along with the results from an elaborate ten-year program of study on heart disease among 3,806 men, has ushered us into the next era of dietary concern. In the past twenty years, the nation's consumption of butter has dropped 30 percent, egg consumption has declined 14 percent, and the average intake of animal fat has plummeted 60 percent. Over the same two decades, deaths from heart disease have declined 30 percent more. But in the face of all these improvements, there is no doubt we are headed into an era of less red meat, butter, bacon, and whole milk consumption.

When I read the results of this study I took an inventory of my own food cabinets and refrigerator contents. I've got a feeling we are going to get accustomed to eating more poultry and fish, or at least I hope so. In our part of the world, fresh fish is not easy to come by, and I never do enjoy the frozen variety. I would rather have salmon loaf, especially the kind that results from the following recipe. As the result of a fishing trip last summer, I have two-dozen cans that I am more than pleased to dedicate to the purpose of this excellent dish.

I do not know if I am nutritionally sound in my observation or not, but it seems to me that the perfect alternative to red meat is tuna fish. It has everything a low-cholesterol diet calls for and none of the problems of meat that come from animal organs. Besides that, there is no end of ways to use tuna fish to the delight of all your guests as well as your family. One of my favorites is the tuna mousse, which I have served scores of times in a fish mold as a special item on a buffet table. Slices

**Chapter Thirty-Three**

of stuffed olives may easily be used to make the eyes of the fish and curly endive makes a good garnish for the edges of the fish platter. Most of all, this tuna mousse is exceptionally good. If you don't believe it, ask nearly anyone who has been to my house for a Christmas buffet or for an after-church supper.

Last summer, Les went fishing with some of his good friends on the lakes near their fishing camp at Frog Rapids, some three hundred miles into Canada beyond International Falls. It was the delight of his life that he caught a fifteen-pound Northern Pike, the largest caught by any of the men in the group. He even carries pictures of that fish in his wallet.

With their legal limit iced down in the trailer, they pulled behind Elmer Brodien's big motor home. The college administrators then proceeded to talk about how they were going to use their fish. Mark Moore, who served as unofficial guide for this fishing excursion, came up with a most unusual recipe for turning Northern Pike into good-quality crab cocktails. This fish dish is not only an alternate to red meat; it is a poor person's answer to the expensive crab cocktails most of us feel we cannot afford in restaurants or at home. Try it—you'll like it.

One of the oldest and best-known institutions in Portland, Oregon, is the main dining room of the Multnomah Athletic Club. They have excellent food at reasonable prices with an atmosphere that fits the hospitality of the Pacific Northwest. Their Bengal Salad is probably the most different and delicious item on their extensive menu. The salad does not change from year to year, just the price, which I am sure must keep pace with the rising cost of seafood. This is probably the single-most popular salad in the Northwest. It is not easy to make, but it is well worth the effort.

### Salmon Loaf

*2 cups red salmon*
*1 cup fine bread crumbs*
*½ cup celery*
*¼ cup green pepper*
*2 tbsp. minced onion*
*1 tbsp. lemon juice*
*1 large can evaporated milk (13 oz.)*
*1 beaten egg*

Combine above ingredients. Bake at 300° for approximately 1 hour. Test as for custard, inserting a knife. It is done when knife edge comes out clean.
Sauce:

*¼ cup mayonnaise*
*1 tbsp. flour*
*¼ tsp. salt*
*⅔ cup evaporated milk (add water to make 1¼ cups)*
*¼ cup sliced stuffed green olives (if desired)*
*¼ cup chopped salted almonds (if desired)*

Combine mayonnaise, flour, salt, and milk mixture. Cook, stirring constantly until thickened. Add olives and almonds (if desired).

### Tuna Mousse

*2 cups water*
*2 envelopes unflavored gelatin*
*2 cans tuna, drained (6½ or 7 oz. each)*
*1 small package cream cheese, cut up (3 oz.)*
*1 small onion, cut up*
*½ cup mayonnaise*
*3 tbsp. lemon juice*
*1¼ tsp. salt*
*1 tsp. sugar*
*1 tsp. grated lemon peel*
*lettuce leaves*
*cherry tomatoes for garnish*

At least 6 hours before serving or day ahead:

In 2-quart saucepan over 1 cup water, sprinkle gelatin. Cook over low heat, stirring constantly, until gelatin is dissolved. In covered blender container at medium speed, blend gelatin mixture, 1 cup water, tuna, and remaining ingredients except lettuce leaves and tomatoes until smooth. Pour into 5-cup mold; refrigerate until set, about 4 hours.

### Minnesota Crab

Boil in salted water (approximately 10 minutes) one medium-sized Northern Pike with onions and celery. Let cool. Remove bones from Northern Pike by turning fish from side to side on wax paper. Be very careful in removing bones because this fish has many very small bones that are hard to find.

*Mixture for Sauce*
*½ cup mayonnaise*
*¼ cup chili sauce*
*½ tsp. Worchestershire sauce*
*¼ cup french dressing*
*¼ cup sweet relish*
*2 tbsp. diced black olives (optional)*

Serve as a salad or crab cocktail.

## Bengal Salad

*1 cup finely diced celery*
*2 oz. sliced water chestnuts*
*½ cup cubed pineapple*
*4 oz. Dungeness crab*
*4 oz. pelled tiny shrimp*
*1 oz. pine nuts*
*½ oz. shredded coconut*

Toss celery, water chestnuts, pineapple, and shrimp meat together lightly. Arrange in lettuce cup. Sprinkle crab meat over the top. Top with Bengal Dressing. Finish with sprinkle of pine nuts and coconut. Serve with slices of fresh fruit and banana bread on an oblong platter.

## Bengal Dressing

*1 cup mayonnaise*
*½ cup sour cream*
*1 cup whipping cream*
*⅛ tsp. curry powder*
*juice of one lemon*
*dash of garlic powder*
*dash of Worchestershire sauce*
*pinch of salt*

Whip cream until fluffy; blend mayonnaise and sour cream. Fold into whipped cream. Gently fold remaining seasonings into mixture. Note: Dressing becomes stronger as it sets.

**Bengal salad is probably the singly most popular salad in the Northwest, not easy to make, but well worth the effort.**

# Mrs. Le Tourneau's Dill Bread

$\mathcal{A}$LTHOUGH Mrs. LeTourneau was married to an industrial giant, she never lost the joy of Christian hospitality and the fulfillment in being her own cook. She even published recipes in the little paper sent out by the LeTourneau Foundation. Some of these were good and some were not so good. But Mrs. LeTourneau's dill bread is the best I have ever tasted.

### Dill Bread

*1 package dry yeast*
*1 cup cottage cheese*
*2 tsp. sugar*
*1 tbsp. minced onion*
*1 tbsp. butter*
*2 tsp. dill seed*
*1 tsp. salt*
*¼ tsp. soda*
*1 unbeaten egg*
*¼ cup water*
*2¼ to 2½ cups flour*

Soften yeast in water. Heat cottage cheese until warm. Add sugar, onion, butter, dill seed, salt, soda, and yeast. Add flour and mix thoroughly. No kneading is necessary. Shape into loaf and place in well-greased bread pan. Let rise until doubled and light. Bake in 350° oven about 45 minutes or until done. Remove from pan immediately and allow to cool.

**Chapter**

**Thirty-Four**

**Mrs. LeTourneau's dill bread is the best I have ever tasted.**

# Quiche Lora Lee

ONE of my favorite late supper specialties is Quiche Lorraine, usually served with either a delicate bibb lettuce salad topped with poppy seed dressing, or for the men present, a sturdier salad that adds avocado, chicken, tomato, chopped egg, and bacon bits to a sturdy bed of lettuce, including Romaine when available. I was startled one day to walk into a restaurant in our community and see my quiche on the menu under the title QUICHE LORA LEE. I understand it was a popular item.

I have depended on this quiche recipe for so many years that I am not sure how I would get along without it. I can only wish it would meet your hospitality needs as much as it has met mine.

### Quiche Lora Lee

*1 cup Bisquick baking mix*
*1/4 cup light cream*
*12 slices bacon (1/2 pound), crisply fried and crumbled*
*1 cup shredded natural Swiss cheese (about 4 oz.)*
*1/3 cup minced onion*
*4 eggs*
*2 cups whipping cream or light cream*
*3/4 tsp. salt*
*1/4 tsp. sugar*
*1/8 tsp. cayenne pepper*

Heat oven to 425°. Stir baking mix and 1/4 cup light cream to a soft dough. Gently smooth dough into a ball on floured cloth-covered board. Knead 5 times. Roll dough 2 inches larger than inverted 9-inch pie pan. Ease into pan and flute edge. Sprinkle bacon, cheese, and onion in crust. Beat remaining ingredients with rotary beater until blended; pour over bacon mixture. Cover edge with 2- to 3-inch strip of alumi-

**I was startled one day to walk into a restaurant in our community and see my quiche on the menu under the title QUICHE LORA LEE.**

num foil to prevent excessive browning; remove foil last 15 minutes of baking. Bake 15 minutes. Reduce oven temperature to 300°. Bake about 35 minutes or until knife inserted 1 inch from edge comes out clean. Let stand 10 minutes before cutting. 6 servings.

## Salad Bowl

For each salad bowl:
>  *1/8 head lettuce, coarsely chopped*
>  *1/8 Romaine, coarsely chopped*
>  *1/4 avocado, diced*
>  *1/3 cup chicken, diced*
>  *1/2 tomato, in wedges*
>  *1/2 oz. hard-cooked egg, finely chopped*
>  *1 oz. crisp bacon finely chopped*
>  *1 lettuce cup, large*

Place chopped greens in lettuce cup. Arrange avocado in center. Surround with diced chicken and ring with tomato sections. Sprinkle with finely chopped egg and bacon, mixed together. Garnish with parsley. Serve with special dressing.

## Special Dressing

Combine:
>  *1 pint french dressing*
>  *1/2 cup Roquefort cheese*
>  *1/2 cup cream*
>  *1 tsp. celery salt*
>  *1 tbsp. Worchestershire*
>  *1 tbsp. chopped chives*
>  *1/2 tsp. white pepper*

## Poppy-Seed Dressing

Combine:
>  *1 1/2 cup sugar*
>  *2 tsp. dry mustard*
>  *2 tsp. salt*
>  *2/3 cup vinegar*
>  *3 tbsp. onion juice*
>  *2 cup salad oil*
>  *3 tbsp. poppy seeds*

# Two Eichenberger Specials

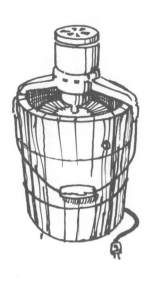

MARGUERITE and Wilbert Eichenberger have exercised more Christian hospitality than any other two people I have ever known. The way we met them, years and years ago, was only the beginning of our lifelong experience of continuing Christian hospitality. Les and I were on the program of the Youth for Christ rally in the Neighbors of Woodcraft Auditorium in Portland, Oregon. We had recently arrived from the Midwest and we honestly knew nobody. I don't even remember how we came to be in charge of the music that night. I do remember that Merv Rozell was the speaker. While Les was singing and I was playing the piano, a young couple from the Friends Church, Wilbert and Marguerite, were sitting in the center of the front row of the balcony. She leaned over to him and said, "I think that is a couple we would like to know." After the meeting that night, they came up to get acquainted and invited us to their house for dinner the following week. And that was how it all started, a pilgrimage of continuing friendship that has lasted until now. Marguerite has always had big houses with lots of space, but she has always felt like her ministry was hospitality with a Christian purpose. The following two recipes homemade ice cream and German pancakes (Dutch babies), have probably been served to more of a roster of Who's Who among evangelical preachers and musicians than any other home recipes in the world.

Wilbert has been the right arm of Dr. Bob Schuller at the Crystal Cathedral in southern California for many years. He is his traveling companion overseas and has served as the director of the Bob Schuller Institute for Ministers. Marguerite is deeply involved in their womens ministries.

**Chapter
Thirty-Six**

**She always felt that her ministry was hospitality with a Christian purpose.**

157

## Homemade Ice Cream

*2 quarts of milk*
*1 pint of whipping cream*
*1 can Eagle Brand sweetened condensed milk (14 oz.)*
*1½ cups sugar*
*dash of salt*
*1 tbsp. vanilla*

Variations:

*5 or 6 bananas according to size*
*nuts to be added after about 10 minutes freezing*
*crushed fresh strawberries, peaches, other fruit, and tinge of food coloring*
*sugar to taste*
*peppermint stick*
*1 package crushed Boston mints*
*peppermint stick candy (leave out some sugar and add pink food coloring).*

Follow manufacturer's directions for freezing in ice cream freezer.

## German Pancakes
### (Dutch Babies)

*3 eggs*
*½ cup flour*
*½ cup milk*
*2 tbsp. melted butter*
*½ tsp. salt*
*lemon wedges*
*confectioners sugar*

In bowl beat eggs with fork or french whip until blended. Add flour to eggs in four additions, beating after each addition until blended and smooth (don't overbeat, though). Add milk in two additions, beating lightly after each. Lightly beat in 2 tablespoons melted butter and ½ teaspoon salt. Thickly grease three 8-inch Pyrex pie plates or two 9-inch. (I find Crisco or vegetable shortening better than butter.) Pour batter into each. Bake in hot oven, 400° for 10 minutes. Reduce oven to 350° and bake 5 minutes more. Serve at once with melted butter, powdered sugar, and lemon wedges. We like sliced strawberries or other fresh fruit on top.

# Hot Spiced Cider

GOT a very nice recipe from Anne Horner, who is the wife of the president of Hanover College. Like all of the rest of us, she was faced with what kind of drink to serve in the fall of the year when iced tea and lemonade are out of season and the heavier holiday recipes for punch bowls are not yet appropriate. Her recipe for hot spiced cider became a favorite of the faculty and students at Hanover as it has for me at Olivet.

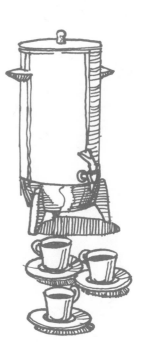

## Hot Spiced Cider

*Use a 30-cup percolator for this recipe.*
*1 gallon apple cider*
*1 cup brown sugar*
*3 oz. can frozen lemonade (½ small can)*
*3 oz. can frozen orange juice concentrate, thawed (½ small can)*
*4 cups water*

In basket where coffee usually is, put 6 cinnamon sticks, 1 tablespoon whole allspice, and 1 tablespoon whole cloves. Plug in percolator and run at full cycle. Makes about 20 cups.

# French Silk Pie

ALL of the chocoholics you know will love you more after you have served them a wedge of French silk pie. Their eyes will light up and they will begin telling you stories of their exploits in the free world of chocolate desserts. But French silk pie can stand the test of comparisons. Be sure to serve it with real whipped cream topped with shavings of chocolate on each piece.

### French Silk Pie

*1¹/₃ cups graham cracker crumbs*
*¹/₃ cup butter, melted*
*1¹/₄ cup (2¹/₂ sticks) butter, softened*
*³/₄ cup sugar*
*2 beaten eggs*
*1 tsp. vanilla*
*1¹/₂ oz. melted semisweet chocolate*

Combine graham cracker crumbs and melted butter in a 9-inch pie pan. Press firmly onto bottom and sides of pan. Refrigerate.

With electric mixer, cream softened butter until smooth. Gradually add sugar and continue beating until very fluffy. Add eggs, vanilla, and chocolate; blend well. Pour into pie shell and chill until ready to serve. May be served cold or at room temperature.

## Chapter Thirty-Eight

**All of the chocoholics you know will love you more after you have served them a wedge of French silk pie. Serve it with real whipped cream topped with shavings of chocolate.**

# Southern Corn Bread

AN Greathouse and her husband Mark who live in Greensburg, Kentucky, have kept us in self-rising white cornmeal mix for a number of years. It contains cornmeal, flour, calcium phosphate, soda, and salt, and comes in ten pound bags. It must be available other places, but Jan and Mark have been our source for a long time. Sometimes they ship it to us and other times they send it by friends, but they always seem to know when we are about to run out. And not only do they have the source, but Jan's recipe is as good or better than any I have ever tried.

Les is from that school of thought that has little concern over the rest of the evening meal as long as hot cornbread is served. He will even eat it cold, or warmed up the next day. Sometimes we take slices from yesterday's supply and toast them after they have been cut down the middle. This makes wonderful bread for jam at breakfast. One of the reasons we like this cornmeal is because it is white, and every southerner knows that white cornmeal is superior to yellow cornmeal.

## Southern Cornbread

*1 cup self-rising cornmeal mix*
*1 cup buttermilk*
*1 egg*
*2 tbsp. corn oil*
*¼ tsp. stoda*
*(1 tsp. sugar, optional)*

(These ingredients are approximations and may need adjusting. The batter should be about the consistency of cake batter.)

Mix. Bake in greased, heated iron skillet. Bake in preheated oven at 450° until golden brown.

One recipe I have used over and over is from the old Moody Press cookbook, *Food for the Body and Soul.* Every time I had three overripe bananas, I would whip up the banana bread on page 54. The boys knew they could cut it and help themselves anytime they saw it cooling on the bread board.

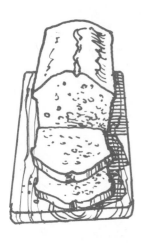

**The boys knew they could cut banana bread and help themselves anytime they saw it cooling on the bread board.**

### Banana Bread

*1 cup sugar*
*½ cup shortening*
*2 eggs*
*3 mashed ripe bananas*
*Pinch salt*
*1 tsp. soda*
*½ tsp. baking powder*
*1¾ cups flour*

Mix in the order given and bake in a slow oven about 50 minutes or until it tests done with a toothpick.

# Homemade Whole Wheat Bread

THE Dallas Baggetts, who are now retired and live in Alabama, have made their own whole wheat bread for years. Les always came home from his visits to their home in Ohio talking about the good bread and the recipe for it that he had brought with him. If you are a bread baker, here is a recipe you will like. It is personalized by the baker.

## Whole Wheat Bread

*1½ cups milk, heated, then cooled*
*1½ cups warm (not hot) water*
*2 packages dry yeast*
*1 tsp. salt*
*⅓ cup vegetable oil*
*¼ cup honey*
*about six cups flour, mixed types if desired*

Heat milk and let cool. Mix thoroughly water and add yeast. To this mixture add salt, vegetable oil, honey and the cooled milk.

Now add enough flour. I use a mixture of whole wheat, white, and stone-ground flour. This gives it a coarser texture and is the reason to use 2 packages of yeast. Add enough to make a dough that is not too stiff, just pliable.

Cover and let rise until doubled. Work down and knead on a lightly floured surface. Form into two loaves. Let rise again and bake in loaf pans at 350° (45-55 minutes) until golden brown.

# A Celebration Supper

## Chapter Forty-One

WHEN our college celebrated its seventy-fifth anniversary a great list of gala events featured some fine food and good fellowship. Most of the festivities were confined to the time between the President's Dinner in early September and the Homecoming events in mid-November.

Les and I decided we would like to celebrate the occasion by inviting a few close friends over for a Sunday night supper after church at the close of Homecoming. Since I knew I would never be up to preparing the food myself, I called on help from one of the best southern cooks I know, Linda Cain, who lives in a tiny Arkansas town called McCrory. She comes from a family of excellent cooks. She knows more about barbecue and chicken and catfish than anyone I have ever known. Her meals are something to behold as well as an experience to be contemplated.

Linda and Don accepted our invitation and came to the Homecoming with an ample supply of genuine barbecued pork and the makings of a celebration supper complete with marinated brisket, southern baked beans, scalloped pineapple, cole slaw, and hummingbird cake for dessert. We invited as many people as we could squeeze around our dining room table, and they are still talking about Linda's barbecue and her scalloped pineapple. If you like this kind of food, her recipes will be worth trying.

**A great list of gala events featured some fine food and good fellowship. They are still talking about LInda's barbecue and her scalloped pineapple.**

## Scalloped Pineapple

*1 large can crushed pineapple (about 20 oz.)*
*2 sticks real butter*
*2 cups sugar*
*3 eggs, beaten*
*4 cups (heaping) white bread, torn into pieces*
*$^1/_3$ cup milk*

Cream butter and sugar. Moisten bread with milk. Stir together. Put into buttered shallow casserole about 9 x 13″. Bake at 325° for 1 hour and 15 minutes.

Linda says that this recipe just doesn't taste right with margarine—it must be pure butter! Makes about 12 servings.

## Marinated Brisket

*1 beef brisket (3 to 5 lbs.)*
*2 cans beef consommé (about 15 oz. each)*
*1 5 oz. bottle soy sauce*
*1 bottle liquid smoke*
*garlic salt, onion salt, pepper*
*barbecue sauce*

Wash brisket in cold water; pat dry with paper towel. Place in roaster and add all ingredients. Cover lightly with foil, not lid. Marinate overnight in refrigerator. Cook 6 to 8 hours at 275° in marinade sauce. Slice with electric knife and put slices into a long casserole dish. Cover with a favorite barbecue sauce, and put back in oven for 45 minutes, uncovered.

## Baked Beans

To one tall can of pork and beans (about 20 oz.) add the following:

*1 bell pepper, chopped*
*1 onion, chopped*
*3 or 4 tbsp. prepared mustard*
*$^1/_2$ cup catsup*
*Sorghum or brown sugar to taste*

Mix well and pour into greased bean pot or baking dish. Sprinkle generously with black pepper. Lay two strips bacon on top and more catsup. Bake at 350° for one hour.

"I really have no recipe for this. I just make it the way my mother does, and she doesn't use a recipe," says Linda.

# Hummingbird Cake

Combine:
> 3 cups all-purpose flour
> 2 cups sugar
> 1 tsp. baking soda
> 1 tsp. salt
> 1 tsp. ground cinnamon

Add:
> 3 eggs, beaten
> 1 cup vegetable oil

Stir until moistened, but do not beat.

Add:
> 1½ tsp. vanilla
> 1 small can crushed pineapple (8 oz.)
> 1 cup chopped pecans
> 2 cups chopped bananas

Stir until mixed, but do not beat. Spoon mixture into 3 greased and floured 9″ round pans. Bake at 350° for 25 to 30 minutes or until a knife comes out clean when inserted in center. Cool in pan for 10 minutes. Remove from pan to cool completely. Spread frosting between layers and on top.

For frosting, combine on low speed of mixer:
> 1 large package cream cheese (8 oz.)
> ½ cup butter
> 16 oz. powdered sugar
> 1 tsp. vanilla

# Sunday Dinner with Dick Jones

URING the week, Dick Jones works from his well-appointed office with a breath-taking view from the sixty-eighth floor of the Sears Tower in Chicago. His position as vice chairperson and chief financial officer for the Sears Roebuck Company demands many skills far from home duties. However, on Sunday mornings, Mr. Jones is in the well-equipped kitchen of their Southwest suburban home. He works on the dinner for Sunday, beginning before Sunday school time with the preparations. The Sunday that we were guests apparently was quite typical. I learned that he first started cooking the dinner to enable his wife Sylvia to get the three children ready for Sunday school. Now they are grown and in college, but the habit continues.

The dinner was delicious and we enjoyed having our plates served. I have had opportunity to eat in some fine French restaurants that were not nearly so delicious and well served as Sunday dinner at the Joneses.

Hors d'oeuvres were in the living room where we enjoyed them and had conversation with Sylvia. The tray included shrimp on toothpicks, cheese squares, and wheat crackers.

The salads were at each place at the table. Bibb lettuce was garnished with a generous amount of pomegranate seeds and the dressing was made with a bacon-fat base, vinegar, water, and sugar.

The plates were beautiful with a delicate and appetizing color combination.

> *Roast fillet of beef with Béarnaise sauce*
> *New potatoes*
> *Julienne carrots in butter sauce*
> *Julienne zucchini*
> *Cauliflower*
> *Garnish of bright parsley*

**The hors d'oeuvres tray included shrimp on toothpicks, cheese squares, and wheat crackers.**

I learned that the fillet of beef was put under the broiler for 15 minutes on each side. Then the beef was placed in the oven to roast for 30 minutes at 350° just before serving. (Allow about ½ lb. per serving.)

Sometimes he serves rice instead of the new potatoes.

The Béarnaise sauce to go with the succulent beef was outstanding. I know that those elegant sauces are time-consuming to make and really take a special knack.

Just as the hot plates were brought, we were also served fresh from the oven, light croissants. I kept asking about and complimenting the Béarnaise sauce and the lovely croissants.

Finally, we were served a smooth chocolate mousse in stemmed glassware. It was delicate and just the right amount of chocolate with a small dollop of whipped cream. After the meal, I had the nerve to suggest, "Mr. Jones, you didn't make those croissants, did you?"

He laughed and said, "Those were from Sara Lee."

Finally, after a visit in their library and discussion on the beautifully bound set of the Great Books collection and of his travels where he had picked up food ideas, we were ready to leave.

I had my coat on and we were right at the door to depart. The host said, "Just one moment, I want to give you something." He presented us with a six-ounce jar of Charlotte Charles Béarnaise sauce.

He said, "Here is my recipe for the sauce you seemed to enjoy."

What a meal. And all Sylvia did was set the table!

# A Midwest French Country Restaurant

## Chapter Forty-Three

BETTY and Gene Dionne operate a French country restaurant in one of the most unlikely places, Momence, Illinois. They have turned the inside of an inauspicious house, which was once their home, into an atmosphere that is as close to French country as you will find outside of France or French-Canada, where the Dionnes first settled before moving on to the Momence area.

You will not find London broil, lake perch, fillets, or dieter's delights in their place. Instead, the diners who come from one hundred miles around will be seated on bentwood chairs at a no-frills table decorated with fresh flowers, while they order from the chalkboard such unusual delights as cassoulet, turkey Orloff, pithivers, tourtiere, quiche Florentine, and occasionally more familiar things like Jambalaya and baked fillet of sole en casserole.

They serve lunch Tuesday through Saturday, and open on Friday evenings for a dinner that is booked two months in advance. Typically generous, Betty and Gene were willing to share two of their prize recipes with me. I almost always order their quiche Florentine because it is the best I have ever had. And you have never really had bread pudding until you enjoy theirs. It does not taste like any bread pudding you've ever had before.

### Quiche Florentine

1 10-inch pastry shell pre-baked for 10 minutes at 425°.
Mix:

    *2 tbsp. butter*
    *1 tbsp. flour*

Add:

    *½ tsp. salt*
    *2 tbsp. finely minced onion*
    *½ tsp. nutmeg*
    *2 tbsp. lemon juice*
    *2 tbsp. Dijon mustard*
    *½ tsp. black pepper*
    *7 to 10 oz. pkg. frozen spinach, thawed and drained*
    *12 oz. half and half*

Next, sprinkle into the pie shell:

    *2 cups grated Swiss cheese*
    *⅓ cup parmesan cheese*

Cover cheese with

    *4 oz. ham, cut into small chunks*

Pour spinach mixture over ham and bake at 350° for 1 hour or until firm.

## Bread Pudding with Orange Sauce

*2 loaves French bread*
*1 quart milk*
*2 tart apples, peeled and sliced*
*1 cup raisins*
*4 eggs*
*1¾ cup sugar*
*2 tbsp. vanilla*
*1½ sticks butter, melted (¾ cup)*
*cinnamon*

Tear bread into small pieces and place in a large mixing bowl (4 quarts of bread). Pour milk over bread and let stand. In a small bowl, beat eggs; add sugar and vanilla. Add apples, raisins, and sugar mixture to bread. Stir to mix thoroughly. Pour some butter into a 9 x 13-inch pan; spread pudding mixture in pan and drizzle rest of butter over top of mixture. Sprinkle with cinnamon. Bake at 350° for approximately 1 hour and 10 minutes. To serve, cut into 15 pieces and top with orange sauce. It is best served warm.

## Orange Sauce

*6 oz. butter*
*1 cup sugar*
*1 egg, beaten*
*2 oz. orange juice*

Melt 6 oz. butter in small pan over low heat. Add 1 cup sugar. Mix until creamy. Remove from heat; quickly add 1 beaten egg. Stir in 2 oz. orange juice. Spoon onto warm bread pudding.

**You have never really had bread pudding until you have tasted this.**

# A Desert Classic

FEBRUARY was R and R time for Les and me. The New England winter had lived up to all of its advance notices. We were ready to spend a few days of rest and recreation with some of our favorite people. The Friesens, Dorothy and Willard, had invited us to their holiday place at Seven Lakes on the desert near Palm Springs. Lois and Shelburne Brown had come up from San Diego and the six of us were enjoying the marvelous experience of letting down without the rigors of deadlines and appointments. In the middle of a green oasis in southern California, the office telephone can seem like a far country. And it was.

One of the things we Christians enjoy most when we let down is the royal fellowship of the dinner table. We went out for lunch and the fellows were getting ready to play golf in the afternoon. But while we were sitting at the table still enjoying our final cup of coffee, we began to talk about the kind of ideal home-cooked meal we would like best if we could just push the right magic buttons. I know that Les and Shelburne knew what a terrific cook Dorothy was. I have no doubt they were harboring hidden thoughts that she might pick up on the idea and come through with a treat of all treats for people who spend lots of time traveling—a good wholesome home-cooked meal. After some discussion we all came to the united conclusion that the ideal home-cooked meal would feature Dorothy's meat loaf and pecan pie. The rest of the menu would be held together with one of her marvelous tossed salads and a large baked potato served with all the accouterments.

In her usual spirit of gracious hospitality, Dorothy agreed to cook the meal and have it ready when the men got back from playing golf. They took off in one direction for the golf course and we took off in the other direction toward a

**One of the things we Christians enjoy most when we let down is the royal fellowship of the dinner table.**

supermarket where all the ingredients for our ideal menu could be brought together at one checkout counter.

That desert classic featuring Dorothy's marvelous meat loaf and pecan pie is a meal we talk about to this day. We must have sat there for at least two hours talking, laughing, reminiscing, and watching daylight turn into dark. It is not possible now to recreate that same atmosphere and set of dynamics again. Time has a way of moving on. But Dorothy's meat loaf and pecan pie are still available for those who have an appreciation for the finer things at the dinner table.

**Dorothy's meat loaf and pecan pie are still available for those who have an appreciation for the finer things at the dinner table.**

## Pecan Pie

*3 eggs*
*2 tbsp. melted butter*
*2 tsp. flour*
*⅛ tsp. salt*
*½ cup sugar*
*1 tsp. vanilla*
*1½ cups Dark Karo syrup*
*1½ cups pecans*

Beat eggs and blend into melted butter. Add dry ingredients and vanilla, Karo, and pecans. Pour in unbaked pie shell. Bake at 400° for 10 minutes and then turn down the oven temperature for 40 minutes to 300°.

## Meat Loaf

*1 lb. hamburger*
*1 egg*
*½ to ¾ cup bread crumbs (reserve a little)*
*1 small can tomato sauce (reserve a little)*
*onion salt*
*garlic salt*
*seasoned pepper*
*½ cup cream or milk*

Put all ingredients in mixing bowl and mix with your hands. Put in greased loaf pan. Sprinkle with reserved bread crumbs mixed with parmesan cheese. Make a line down the middle with reserved tomato sauce or catsup. Bake at least 1 hour at 325-350°.

# Famous Senate Restaurant Bean Soup

SOME things cannot be bought even if you have the money. One of these is a meal in the Senator's Dining Room at the Capitol Building in Washington D.C. From childhood I have heard stories about this dining room and the famous bean soup served to the waves of elected officials who come and go through those exclusive doors. But it never crossed my mind I would ever go there.

Then one day, Les and I visited the Senate in session at the Capitol. I don't know yet how the chaplain of the Senate knew we were there. But without warning, there was a courteous tap on the shoulder and the security guard at the door asked us to step out into the corridor to see the chaplain, Edward Elson. I had heard about him and knew that he was the famous pastor of the National Presbyterian Church who built the campus of buildings that houses their ministry in Washington D.C. I also had read a quote from him that I liked. He said that after spending more than ten years in constructing buildings and attending building committees, he knew when he died that he had gone to the wrong place if he woke up in a building committee meeting. Now we were to see him face to face.

Dr. Elson was gracious in every way and invited us almost immediately to join him for lunch in the Senator's Dining Room. I know he must have thought I was naive as I looked at the many faces I had recognized through the media. So often I had to inquire of him about their identity. But before we left the restaurant, I not only had a bowl of their famous bean soup, but I had obtained through him a copy of the recipe. I hope you will enjoy it.

## The Famous Senate Restaurant Bean Soup

*2 lbs. Michigan navy beans*
*4 quarts hot water*
*1½ lbs. smoked ham hocks*
*1 chopped onion*
*butter*
*salt and pepper to taste*

Wash navy beans and run through hot water until beans are white. Put beans on the fire with 4 quarts of hot water. Boil ham hocks slowly 3 hours in a covered pot. In small saucepan braise chopped onion in a little butter; when light brown, add to soup. Remove ham hocks and let cool. Dice ham and return to soup. Remove 2 cups of beans; puree and return to soup. When ready to serve season with salt and pepper. Serves 8.

# Buckeyes

## Chapter Forty-Six

HAVE always associated peanuts with the South. George Washington Carver made them meaningful, the Planter's Peanut Company made them popular, and President Carter gave them status. But one of the best peanut-butter recipes I ever tasted does not come from Georgia or Alabama, but from New England. Janice Nielson, who is in the third generation of a wonderful New England family, gave me this recipe, which will make 200 peanut-butter cups. That may seem like a lot to you until you have put them on the table for a disappearing act like you have never seen before.

### Buckeyes

*1 lb. butter*
*2 lbs. peanut butter*
*3 lbs. sugar*

Mix and form into walnut-size balls. With toothpick, dip balls in melted mixture of:

*1 pkg. (12 oz.) chocolate chips*
*½ slab of paraffin (2 oz. piece)*

Leave top of ball free of chocolate. Cool on waxed paper. Yield 200.

**Buckeyes will do a disappearing act like you have never seen before.**

# Breakfast Casserole

COMPANY breakfast is one of my favorite things. First of all, I like to get up early. Not many people specialize in serving breakfast on a grand scale. The guests are always brighter and to come over to my house at the beginning of the day rather than the end pleases me. Furthermore, breakfast is our favorite meal of the day.

Sometimes I serve the traditional ham, bacon, and scrambled eggs, but add fried bananas and southern baking powder biscuits with ample supplies of jams and jellies. Another favorite item is a big red baked apple. But one of the few specialty dishes I know about that rates candles at breakfast time is a unique breakfast casserole. It has enough substance to handle the heartiest of the big eaters, and served with a compote of fresh fruit and lots of hot coffee, it is always a hit.

Another crowd pleaser at breakfast is hot bran muffins, right out of the oven. The good thing about this recipe is that the mixture may be kept covered in the refrigerator and baked as needed. I often bake six of these for breakfast from my supply of dough, which can last up to six weeks. Besides breakfast, these bran muffins are especially convenient and helpful when unexpected guests drop by.

### Breakfast Casserole

*6 eggs (beaten)*
*1 pound sausage (cooked and drained)*
*3 slices of bread (broken in pieces)*
*2 cups milk*
*1 tsp. mustard*
*1 tsp. salt*
*1 cup shredded cheddar cheese*

Combine ingredients and put into greased glass baking dish. Bake at 350° for 35-45 minutes. Can be prepared the night before.

## Bran Muffins

*1 box raisin bran*
*1 quart buttermilk*
*5 cups flour*
*5 tsp. baking soda*
*2 tsp. salt*
*3 cups sugar*
*1 cup vegetable oil*
*4 eggs well beaten*

Mix all ingredients and bake at 400° in muffin tins.

**Another crowd-pleaser at breakfast is hot bran muffins, right out of the oven.**

## Subject Index

Some old, some new . . . some tried, all true . . . get out the apron, get out the pan . . . stir and mix as fast as you can!

| Rhubarb Pie | 143 |
| Pecan Pie | 176 |
| Philadelphia Cream Cheese Pie | 140 |

## Salads

| Bengal Salad | 152 |
| Chicken Salad Supreme | 127 |
| Salad Bowl | 156 |

# Index of Recipes

*Notes*

# Notes